THE BOY WHO DISAPPEARED

VALERIE NETTLES

THE BOY WHO DISAPPEARED

The true story
of every mother's
worst nightmare...

JOHN BLAKE

Published by John Blake Publishing,
The Plaza,
535 Kings Road,
Chelsea Harbour,
London SW10 0SZ

www.facebook.com/johnblakebooks
twitter.com/jblakebooks

This edition first published in 2019

Paperback ISBN: 978 1 78946 071 1
Ebook ISBN: 978 1 78946 093 3

British Library Cataloguing-in-Publication Data:

A catalogue record for this book is available from the British Library.

Design by www.envydesign.co.uk

Printed and bound in Great Britain by Clays Ltd, Elcograf S.p.A.

1 3 5 7 9 10 8 6 4 2

John Blake Publishing is an imprint of Bonnier Books UK
www.bonnierbooks.co.uk

CONTENTS

INTRODUCTION
BY BRONAGH MUNRO

'We are stuck in limbo…. We just can't go on with our lives, we just want Damien to come home.'

'The worst thing is not knowing where he is. It's exhausting. I don't have a marker for where my baby is. I don't have a grave and I don't have closure.'

'Finding his body or what is left of it would be a gift. It might not end the distress but if I could place him somewhere, instead of thinking of every awful thing that might have happened to him and wondering if he cried for us, if someone beat him, murdered him, if he knew what was going on, did he call for us …?'

Valerie Nettles, 2015

WHEN I FIRST SPOKE TO VALERIE NETTLES, HER WORDS, SADNESS and frustration made a huge impact on me. Behind her grief, there was a determination and resilience that I immediately admired and responded to.

She was a fighter and I understood that she could not move on with her own life until she found the answers to what had happened to her son Damien. She was caught in limbo, I wanted to help her. I felt I could. But I was under no illusion at the task ahead.

On 2 November 1996, sixteen-year-old Damien had left the family home, on the Isle of Wight, headed into the small town of Cowes, for a night out, and never came back. He just disappeared.

Today, almost twenty-three years later, police still haven't been able to explain what happened to Damien. They say over a thousand people have been involved in their investigation; hundreds of witness statements have been taken and thousands of documents reviewed. Yet the case remains unsolved, his body hasn't been found and no one has been charged with his murder.

In October 2015, I was part of a BBC team of four that moved to the Isle of Wight to investigate Damien's disappearance. We rented an out-of-season holiday home and spent three months working day and night on the case. In total, I worked for a year on the case.

Up to that point, the police with all their resources had been working on the case for twenty years. Other journalists, councillors, friends and private detectives had been involved with no success. There was no crime scene, no body and only circumstantial evidence to follow. The case wasn't just cold, it was frozen.

The jungle drums started beating the moment we arrived on the island, word soon spread and local residents began greeting us by name. We became a regular fixture in the town of Cowes. People were friendly. Everyone we spoke to told us a version of the story of Damien Nettles, 'The Boy Who Disappeared'.

That was the problem, the island was awash with theories about what they believed had happened. It was difficult to decipher if people's recollections were something they directly witnessed. Or if it was just more hearsay, an opinion based on what they had been told or what they had read in the paper, passed onto Valerie in good faith?

We were seasoned investigative journalists used to hearing all manner of accusations, used to sifting through truths and half-truths to get to the facts underneath. I'd spent years working on old cases. Murders, paedophilia, allegations of police wrongdoing and informants were my stock and trade. Before that I'd been a police officer for nearly ten years.

But in Damien's case, even I found it was no easy task to sort fact from fiction. The lack of physical evidence and the absence of a crime scene was always a difficult starting point. How Valerie has dealt with it all, I will never know.

We were prepared to explore all avenues but we wanted hard evidence, we wanted to prove or disprove the many stories Valerie had been told. Nothing was off the table.

It has always been important to view Damien's disappearance in the context of the time it happened. It was 1996, there were virtually no mobile phones and the internet as we know it was only emerging. You planned your nights out in person and communicated via landlines. Social media as we know it didn't exist. In today's world we would have started by examining anything and everything to do with Damien and his family's digital footprint. We would have searched his phone history, combed his social media accounts, pored over photos, text messages and email accounts, looking for any piece of evidence no matter how small – Who was he? What were his interests? Who had he spent time with that night or the weeks prior to his disappearance? – gathering details to stitch together into a detailed tapestry of Damien's life.

But we didn't have that in this case. The police investigation would not have been able to rely on any of this information either. It was a different time.

From the outset we were keen to meet with the police, to work with them. Disappointingly they chose not to engage with us or share any information that might have helped.

So all we had to go on was news reports from the time, and thousands of uncategorised emails that had passed between the Nettles family, police, and witnesses over the past two decades. Valerie's emails became an unofficial chronology of everything that has happened in relation to Damien's case.

I spoke to many locals, business owners, and friends of the family, as well as anyone who had been spoken to by the police; all remember the family searching for Damien after he went missing. Many who spoke to me told me that they felt that the police hadn't done enough. They felt the police investigation had been too narrow in its scope in the early days. Looking back I share Valerie's frustration, as that was the time when people's memories were freshest and most evidence could have been gathered. Some told us they believed the initial investigation by the police was only in one direction.

But we also spoke off-the-record to ex-cops who worked the beat in Cowes back in the 1990s, who say they did everything they could after Damien disappeared. They told us Operation Ridgewood commenced immediately. An incident room was set up with a team of dedicated officers, searches were carried out, and people of interest were spoken to. We were never given an opportunity to examine the files so I have no way of knowing for definite what was or what was not done in those irreplaceably valuable hours and days when Damien was first discovered missing.

Opinions aside, the facts remain; we know vital evidence from this time was not retained by the police. Valerie believes this has hampered the case. And I agree. An opportunity to identify witnesses and suspects alike was gone. Just like Damien.

Again the argument of whether information was lost accidentally or deliberately destroyed cannot be settled as the paperwork relating to the tapes has never been seen. Having been a police officer myself, I understand the strict procedures that should govern the chain of evidence in relation to exhibits. I find it incomprehensible that this could have happened and the officer responsible only receive a warning.

* * *

Back in 1996, like now, the Isle of Wight was renowned for its sailing regatta, music festivals and beautiful scenery. Cowes in particular is overrun in the summer months by tourists and the yachting crowd that flock to the island.

The locals rely on the tourism for income but it is like any small seaside town, scratch the surface and you will find that the welcome is begrudging. The population explosion in the summer months puts a strain on the island's infrastructure and resources, but the income from the tourism is vital to its economy.

It was winter when we stayed on the island so we avoided the influx of tourists, giving the locals valuable time to talk to us. It allowed us to get a sense of the town at the very time of year that Damien disappeared. In fact, one of our first filming days was a vigil on the anniversary of his disappearance.

During those months we spent night after night in Cowes, retracing Damien's last steps, walking the streets, getting a feel for the town under the cloak of early darkness. It always struck me how tiny the town was, how narrow the streets, and how easily voices carried late in the evening when the streets began to empty. All of the sightings of Damien were in areas that were well lit and overlooked by windows. It became impossible to believe that anything could happen in this town without it being seen or heard by someone. It is a place where everyone knows everyone else's business.

But could the web of rumours around the disappearance of Damien Nettles ever be unpicked? We tried. In the absence of an active police investigation our aim was to help Valerie to identify what had potentially happened or not happened to Damien that night. But it was important to be realistic. The last thing I wanted was to give Valerie more false hope.

In Damien's case there were nearly as many theories about what happened to him as the number of years he had been gone. Did he drown, did he go missing, did he run away, was he killed and if he was killed, who killed him…?

We explored and discounted other stories that claimed Damien simply left of his own accord, that he had been kidnapped and taken off the island by boat against his will, and that he was killed by a paedophile. None of these appeared to have any substance.

What I was told repeatedly was that Damien was a happy, content boy who loved life. From what his friends told us, he appeared to have no reason to run away. Something just didn't fit. From day one, we couldn't find anything unusual about the days leading to Damien's disappearance. And all evidence suggests that he vanished in circumstances that were unforeseen by him.

Trawling Valerie's emails for names, we hunted witnesses down, travelling all over the island to find and speak to people who had sent her messages. Valerie was desperate for us to test the veracity of their stories in person, something she had never been able to do. Something the police for whatever reason hadn't always done.

In the absence of other evidence we knocked on doors. We slept a few feet from an investigation room, where potential suspects, theories and maps lined the walls.

We spoke to anyone we could find who worked in Cowes back in 1996, people who had worked in the bars and restaurants, door staff, taxi drivers, sailors, fishermen, and even ex-police officers.

During the day we lived out of our car, spending hours, even days, waiting to catch a glimpse of or better still be able to speak to potential eyewitnesses and suspects. Locals were friendly but there was definitely the feeling that we were visitors to their island.

I believe the passage of time has both helped and hindered Damien's case. Friendships and relationships have ended, loyalties have changed and consciences have grown. People were perhaps more prepared to talk to us now, but by this time it was tough to substantiate their allegations and claims. And even tougher for them to recall what memories were their own or those gleaned from the copious amount of local news reports published. Nothing could be taken at face value. Everything we were told, we checked.

More often than not the theories Val had been sent turned into false leads. But identifying that was still an achievement, it was one more false hope to cross off Valerie's list. And a step closer to the truth.

In the end, the story brought us far from the postcard image of the island, into a darker world inhabited by the island's heroin addicts, drug dealers and police informants. A place were two things mattered most: survival and money for another hit. A place that had no consideration for a mother's grief.

It was a world we found intrinsically linked with Damien's case. Repeatedly names from the islands drug fraternity were given to us when we asked what had happened to Damien. The circumstances varied but the names remained constant. Too constant to ignore.

When we tried to test the veracity of this information with those who knew Damien back then, do I believe we were always told the truth? No, not for one minute.

Witnesses had spoken to police repeatedly by the time we arrived. They had already established their stories. It was frustrating. Many things we were being told by them, we knew to be at odds with this fresh information.

We learned that in 1996 the Isle of Wight was a very different place. Two separate worlds co-existed on that small island. Drugs were a serious problem. Not just cannabis and acid – the drugs typically associated with the mid 1990's rave and island party scene – heroin was taking hold and the island's drug users had yet to find out just how deadly the consequences would be. Many of those named and later arrested in relation to Damien's disappearance were consumed by this new deadlier drug. Many of them sold it, and some were dead from overdoses by the time we picked up the case. With them died valuable opportunities to gather evidence.

Over time it became obvious from the witnesses that we spoke to that in 1996 the drugs trade on the island had become a launch point for getting drugs into the UK. These drugs were easily accessible to all ages. Various houses dotted around

Cowes at the time were used as drug houses, somewhere anyone could buy and use without being hassled. We were repeatedly given information that led me to believe that Damien's world had collided, however accidentally, with this darker side of the island and its criminals.

I believe this collision of worlds gave rise to a sequence of unforeseen events that led to his disappearance. For legal reasons, so much of this never made the film. But we shared it all with Valerie hoping it would provide some answers in the absence of being able to find her son.

In making the series, bringing Valerie face to face with some of these witnesses and criminals was a tough decision for me. But I was convinced it was much tougher for them to look a grieving mother in the face and lie than a journalist. Turns out I was wrong.

Valerie was incredibly brave during those meetings, as she has been throughout the last two decades years.

Our BBC investigation was just a small chapter in Valerie's search to find out what happened to Damien that night. But I absolutely believe she will one day get the answers she needs to move on. It was an absolute privilege to share part of this long hard journey with her and her family.

In my experience, in older cases, it is the sheer determination of the family and their resilience in the face of unbelievable adversity that solves the case. Only a family member – in this case, a mother – could have the resolve to keep going long after everyone else has quit.

It is this quiet intractable strength, that I witnessed Valerie draw on so often, that I have always felt will finally uncover what really happened to Damien Nettles on that fateful night.

THE SOLENT

Baring Road

Northwood
Park

GURNARD

Woodvale Road

The Nettles'
family home

Baring Road

B3325

1. Grange Road, East Cowes, where Damien went to a party with
   his friend Chris.
2. Alldays, Grange Road, where Damien bought cider.
3. The ferry crossing connecting East Cowes and Cowes.
4. The Duke of York pub
5. Yorkies chip shop – Damien went inside at 10pm and 11.30pm.
6. The Arcade
7. The Fountain pub
8. Here, Chris and Damien parted company by the steps to
   Northwood Park at 10.30pm.
9. Damien heads back towards town and witnesses see him on
   the High Street at 10.45pm and at the Harbour Lights pub at
   11.10pm. A member of staff says they saw Damien there again
   at 11.45pm.
10. Damien is seen at the Three Crowns pub at 11.20pm.
11. The bus stop where Damien got onto a bus at 11.52pm, asking
    to go to Cowes. He thanks the driver and gets off the bus.
12. Last known sighting of Damien at 12.02am, 3rd November.

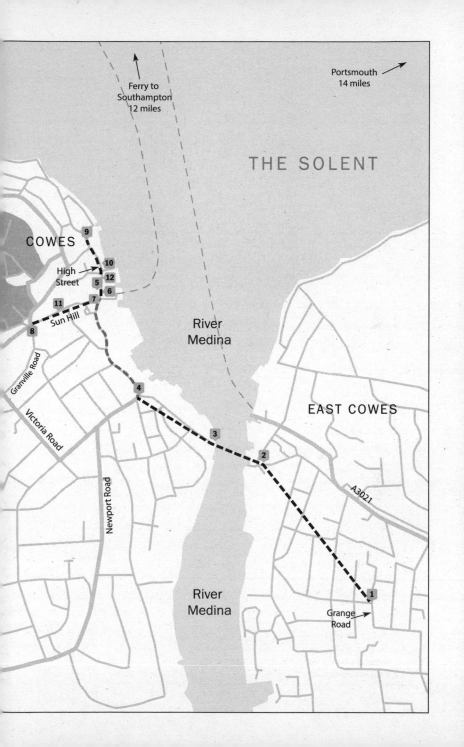

THE SOLENT

Portsmouth
14 miles

Ferry to
Southampton
12 miles

COWES

9

10

High
Street

5

12

6

7

11

Sun Hill

8

Granville Road

Victoria Road

River
Medina

4

Newport Road

3

2

EAST COWES

A3021

River
Medina

1

Grange
Road

CHAPTER ONE

THERE WAS NOTHING REMARKABLE OR DIFFERENT ABOUT THAT Sunday. It was a typical grey and blustery November morning on the Isle of Wight. My husband Ed and I had been up for a little while, preparing breakfast and getting on with the usual Sunday chores in our family home on Woodvale Road in the village of Gurnard.

Our youngest, nine-year-old Melissa, was already up and buzzing around the house playing with her toys and watching cartoons but, as usual, our two sons, James, twelve, and Damien, sixteen, were yet to surface from their bedrooms. I'd already heard James stirring, probably roused by the sound of the house coming to life, or perhaps the smell of breakfast cooking, but I hadn't heard a peep from Damien. No surprise, really. He'd been out the night before.

I sent Melissa on a mission. 'Go and wake Damien up,' I said with a smile.

Off she bounded, taking the stairs two at a time as she dashed past James, who was shuffling sleepily in the other direction. He walked into the kitchen and sat down at the table. I hadn't even had time to say good morning before Melissa burst back into the room.

'He's not in bed, Mum,' she said, a confused expression evident on her face. 'Damien's not in his room.'

'Are you sure?' I asked, frowning. 'Is he in the bathroom, maybe?'

Melissa shook her head.

How strange, I thought, marching up the stairs. I hadn't heard him come in, but then his curfew was midnight and I'd gone to bed before then. Ed had stayed up until almost twelve, expecting him to come through the door any minute, but he'd nodded off too. It wasn't that he'd never come home later than we agreed, but he did always call me to let me know.

'Damien,' I called, just in case he was elsewhere in the house. No reply.

Entering his room, it was clear he'd not been home. The sheets on his bed were still smoothed back neatly and his pillows undented. His childhood teddy, Berry, was propped up in his usual place on the bed alongside Woggle, a gangly stuffed dog that had previously belonged to his Auntie Sally. The new grey school trousers we'd bought while shopping in Newport the day before still hung on his cupboard door and a stack of school textbooks was piled up on his desk. He'd told me he had a lot of studying to do before school on Monday.

Even more reason that he should be home by now.

In fact, scanning his room, everything was exactly as he'd left it when he'd hopped in his dad's car to get a lift over to his best friend, Chris Boon's house. That was at 7pm. He must still be there, I rationalised. What other explanation was there?

They'd been going to a party over in East Cowes with Chris's younger brother Davey. He hadn't said, but I assumed there might have been alcohol there. We knew they occasionally sneaked a few ciders. I'd told Damien off for it in the past. He was tall for his age and a handful of shops were a little lax when it came to checking ID, so of course they tried their luck. Maybe he'd had a few too many; ended up a little worse for wear . . .

I could have called Chris there and then, but I looked at the clock. It was only 8:30am. He was probably sleeping it off. There was every chance in the next hour or so we'd get a sheepish and hung-over call from him, explaining his whereabouts. While my gut told me that something was amiss, I didn't want to overreact. At sixteen, Damien was still a child in our eyes, but we were also aware he was on the cusp of adulthood. We didn't want to cramp his style.

'It is a Sunday,' said Ed. 'Let's wait a little longer to call.'

For the next two hours I almost wore the carpet through, pacing around the house and looking out of the front window, hoping to see him walking up the path.

Nothing.

The anxiety began to wear me down as the minutes ticked by. Where was he? I stared and stared at the phone, willing it to ring.

Still nothing.

By the time late morning arrived, I couldn't take it any more. I grabbed the telephone and punched in Chris's number. The phone seemed to ring for an eternity before there was a click and I heard Chris's voice answer.

'Hello?' he said.

'Hello, Chris. It's Valerie, Damien's mum,' I said, relief washing over me.

Chris was home and awake, so Damien must be with him, I reasoned with myself.

'Oh, er, hi, Mrs Nettles,' he said.

I frowned. Did he sound surprised, or nervous? I wondered if I might have caught him on the hop, if he knew Damien had stayed out late without our permission. Anything except the fact that he wasn't there.

'Is Damien with you, Chris?' I asked.

'Here?' he replied, puzzled.

'Yes, at your house,' I spelled out.

Chris paused. I prayed he was searching for a good excuse or cover story. Then he replied.

'No. I left him in town at about half past ten last night. We were both heading home . . .' he said, trailing off. 'Did he not come home?'

My heart skipped a beat. He'd left Chris well before he was due home. So where was he? I felt panic building but I didn't want to alarm Chris. He was only a kid himself, after all.

'He's not been home yet,' I said, trying to maintain composure as the knot in my stomach tightened. 'Was he okay when you left him?'

'Yes,' he replied, stuttering slightly. 'I mean, we'd had a few drinks. Not loads. He seemed fine.'

A few? How? He'd only had a few pounds on him. Questions swirled in my head but I calmed myself. I didn't want anyone to worry about getting in trouble. I just wanted to know where Damien was. There must be a logical explanation.

'Can you call round your other friends?' I asked. 'See if anyone has seen him?'

'Of course,' he said.

'Let me know if you hear anything,' I insisted. 'Anything at all.' I hung up and turned to Ed. 'We have to call everyone,' I said. 'Something is wrong. Someone will surely know where he is.'

A flurry of phone calls followed. Ed and I, and even James, rang our way through our phone book, asking everyone we knew if they'd seen Damien. We even rang our eldest daughter Sarah, who was at university in Portsmouth. There were only a few years between them, and they'd always been close, so it wasn't inconceivable that Damien might have decided to get a boat to the mainland to see her. That said, he wouldn't have had the money for the boat and he'd seen her only a few days earlier. When I got hold of Sarah, my thoughts were confirmed.

'He's not here,' she said. 'I haven't heard from him either. Should I come home?'

'No,' I said. 'He might turn up there. We'll let you know when we hear anything.'

'Okay,' she said.

I could tell in her voice that she felt what I was feeling – deep unease. Damien wasn't a naughty kid. He was close to his family and he was always in contact. Something just wasn't right.

We called everyone we knew. Every last person. No one had seen Damien anywhere. Nor had they heard from him since the previous evening. With rational explanations slipping away, my mind turned to darker thoughts. What if something had happened after he'd left Chris? Living on a small island we'd always felt safe. Everyone knew everyone and we usually kept an eye out for one another. Despite the rising tide of fear creeping,

I reassured myself that there would be a logical explanation. But then nature reminded me of risks that were harder to avoid. I glanced anxiously out of the window at the sea, but I couldn't allow my mind to consider that possibility yet. The grey sky was turning black as thick clouds rolled in and rain began to cascade down.

I shuddered. What if he'd fallen and hurt himself? Somehow headed towards the cliffs at Thorness Bay and slipped? Especially if he'd been drinking. He might be out there somewhere, alone and injured. Scared and calling out for his mum and dad. The thought made my heart hurt. Tears welled up in my eyes. I just wanted to find him. I couldn't sit around any longer.

'I'm going out to look for him,' I announced, leaping to my feet and grabbing my coat. As I reached the door, I turned to Ed. 'Stay here in case he comes home.'

'Can I come, Mummy?' Melissa pleaded. 'I'll help you look for Damien.'

'You stay here with Daddy,' I said, willing my voice not to betray my emotions. 'I won't be gone long.'

By this time James had wandered back to his bedroom. To be honest, I was glad he was out of the way. I knew from the look on Ed's face that he was entering panic mode, just like me. We didn't want the children to see fear taking a hold of us.

I jumped into our white Mazda, pulled the door shut, clicked on my seat belt and revved the engine to life in one swift movement. As I drove, I fought to stay positive. I told myself over and again that I'd spot him somewhere. See him walking back towards home. Truth be told, it felt more like a prayer.

Please let me see him somewhere.

At six foot three inches tall and thin as a rake, he was pretty hard to miss at the best of times. Still, I drove slowly and purposefully, thoroughly scoping out all the usual routes he took home. Every time a human outline appeared my heart leapt into my throat, only to sink again when I realised it wasn't Damien.

Too short. Too old. Too young.

The black clouds continued to close in around the car and the usually picturesque, leafy streets of the island lost their lustre. The rain pounded heavily on the ground. I couldn't help but worry that the black fleece he'd pulled on as he left the house would be soaked through by now. He'd be frozen, wet, miserable and possibly alone. Or worse, said a little voice in my head. It was accompanied by a heavy feeling – one of dread and fear that weighed across my shoulders. A sense of impending doom. I tried to shake it off. I was a worrier.

Come on, Val, it'll be fine. He'll be fine.

After scouring all the streets that made up routes Damien could take to get home with no luck, I decided to head to Gurnard Pines.

The Pines, as it was known locally, was an old holiday camp where Damien had worked during the summer. It was situated in Gurnard and reminiscent of an old Butlin's, the kind that would be filled with jolly campers in the 1950s and '60s. That glory was long faded now. All that was left was a mix of caravans and stone chalets, alongside more recently built timber holiday huts, with a few stark amenities – a pool, clubhouse and restaurant. It was pretty basic and quiet out of season, but busy during the holidays, as it was well located for families who wanted to explore the island: 'grockles', as natives to the island called them.

But those of us who lived there knew there was a darker undercurrent to the place, if you scratched below the thin veneer. Mixed in among the visitors were locals who leased chalets during the winter months but had to vacate them during the summer season. They were odd characters, many there because their relationships had broken down. It seemed a strange way of life to me. And the site owners? Well, there had been more than a few rumours around town about their dodgy behaviour. I never dwelled on it too much, though; it was all hearsay after all.

Sarah had worked at The Pines before university and had never had any trouble so, despite everything, it seemed like the ideal part-time job for Damien too. He'd taken to it like a duck to water and made new friends immediately, in particular one lad called Jon Meeks, a bartender at the camp who was a couple of years older than him. I'd not been able to get hold of him on the phone, so I'd decided to drop by to see if I could find him. Maybe he'd know where Damien was.

My skin prickled in anticipation as I headed up the driveway into The Pines. You see, Jon wasn't like Damien's other friends from school in Cowes or nearby Carisbrooke. I didn't like to say it, as I'd only met him a handful of times, but he made me uneasy. He was pleasant enough, but he seemed more streetwise compared to Damien's other friends, who were still quite daft and immature. It wasn't because he was living in a caravan at The Pines. It wasn't even because Damien had told me he'd bragged about drugs a few times. That could have just been teenage bravado. It was because, rightly or wrongly, I felt he'd already led Damien astray once.

A few weeks earlier, Damien had asked if it was okay for him to get the boat over to Portsmouth for the weekend. He'd told me that he and Jon wanted to go and see a rock concert.

'He's got a friend we can stay with in town,' Damien had pleaded.

Ed and I were reticent. 'We don't know these people,' I said.

'But *I* do, Mum,' he pushed.

We laboured over the decision. He was our little boy. But he was also growing up. With that in mind, we agreed that he could go. But only if he promised to be home by Sunday night. If he needed anything he was to contact Sarah, who lived nearby.

Damien was over the moon. When Saturday came, off he went, happy as Larry. I, on the other hand, was a wreck. I barely slept a wink while he was away. This was just part of him growing up, I told myself, over and over. He'll be fine. Letting go was hard. But I knew it had to happen sometime.

Saturday night passed. Sunday came and went. There was no sign of Damien.

Another sleepless night passed. When he still hadn't returned home by Monday morning, Ed and I were frantic. I knew he was due on shift, so I called The Pines to see if he'd gone straight into work from off the boat.

'I'm sorry,' said the man on the end of the line. 'Damien didn't turn up for work.' Jon had been a no-show too.

Surprise, surprise.

By lunchtime I was ready to send out a search party, but then I'd heard the click of the front door and Damien tiptoed into the hall several hours after he'd been due home.

'Where the heck have you been?' Ed demanded.

'We've been worried sick,' I added. 'You were meant to be home yesterday.'

At first, Damien stared at his shoes and apologised sheepishly. But after a few cups of tea and some gentle coaxing, the real story unfolded. Turns out, Damien had met a girl while working at the camp. Her name was Gemma and she was on holiday there with her family. She and Damien had fallen for one another and they'd stayed in touch after she'd returned home to Suffolk. In fact, they'd become boyfriend and girlfriend. There had never been a rock concert in Portsmouth. Or a friend of Jon's that they could stay with. It had all been a ruse so Damien and Jon could go to Suffolk to see Gemma and her friend.

I was shocked and disappointed. He had never behaved like this before. We'd always been open and fair. He'd never had any need to lie. I couldn't help but think that this Jon lad had something to do with it all.

'Why didn't you just tell us?' I asked. *Did Jon put you up to this?* I wanted to add, but I bit my lip.

Damien shrugged, looking awkward and embarrassed. 'I just wanted to see her,' he said. 'I didn't think you'd let me go.'

I sighed loudly. 'Damien, if you like this girl I'm sure we could have found a way for you to see her,' I said. 'One that didn't involve you sneaking around.'

He hung his head and nodded. 'I'm sorry, Mum,' he said. 'Sorry, Dad.'

I threw my arms around him and hugged him tightly. I knew he was genuinely sorry. Anyway, how could I stay angry when I was so utterly relieved? My baby was home and that was all that mattered.

'It's okay,' I said. 'It's done now. Just remember to always talk to us first.'

I really felt like our message had sunk in. There was nothing he couldn't talk to us about. But as I pulled into The Pines car park, I wondered if maybe I'd been wrong. Maybe Jon had somehow managed to talk him into another silly escapade?

I pulled my hood up and ran across the car park towards the rows of caravans, lashed by the rain as I went. I made a beeline for Jon's caravan and rapped urgently on the door. A moment passed and he appeared.

'Jon,' I said. 'I'm looking for Damien. Is he here?'

For a moment he stared, puzzled by the dripping, breathless heap standing before him. But as Damien's name sank in, a look of recognition crossed his face.

'Oh, hello, Mrs Nettles,' he said. 'No, Damien's not here.'

As my eyes connected with his, I heard something in the background – a gentle thud, like he wasn't alone in there.

'Have you seen him at all today?' I asked again, craning my neck to try and look around the door.

'No,' Jon replied, shaking his head. 'I haven't seen him for a few weeks, not since . . .' His voice tailed off and I raised an eyebrow. I knew what he was about to say: 'Not since we went to Suffolk.'

I eyeballed Jon and spoke again. 'Are you sure you haven't seen him?' I pushed, one last time. The expression on my face obviously betrayed me – he could tell I didn't trust him.

'Honestly, Mrs Nettles, I haven't seen him at all,' he said, raising his hands slightly, almost in submission. 'But I can ask around.'

I stared for a moment longer, then nodded. At this point I had no choice but to trust him. I needed to keep looking for Damien. I handed him our home phone number, written on a scrap of paper.

'Call me if you hear anything. It doesn't matter what time it is,' I said. I leapt back into the car and sped home.

I could see Ed's face at the window as I drew nearer. Maybe he had better news? I smiled hopefully at him but he just shook his head. I gestured for him to get in the car. My parents were home with the children now, so Ed could join the hunt. Two pairs of eyes would be better than one.

For two hours we crawled up and down street after street, from the quiet residential streets of Gurnard and Carisbrooke, to Cowes town centre and the coastal areas. By early afternoon, still having no news or sight of Damien, we drove home and sat silently for a moment outside our house. The wind was howling and the driving rain meant even our front door was nothing more than a blurry outline. My stomach churned as I imagined Damien out there on his own. I just knew something was wrong. The voice that I'd been trying to subdue all day started roaring in my head.

What if he's fallen somewhere? What if he's lying injured, unable to reach help? What if he was calling out for us, cold and scared?

No boundaries Damien tested would have pushed us this far, I was certain of it. I turned to Ed.

'Something's not right,' I said, shaking my head. 'Should I go to the police?'

Ed nodded. 'Yes. I think so.' We'd exhausted every possibility we could think of. Now we needed help to find our son.

CHAPTER TWO

DECISION MADE, I DASHED BACK INSIDE THE HOUSE. AS I DID, Melissa appeared at my waist.

'Not now,' I said. 'Mummy has to go somewhere.'

'I want to come with you,' she said, throwing her arms around me and clinging on for dear life. As her little face looked up at me I could see she was scared and worried. Ed and I were trying our best to remain calm, but by now I was sure that the fear and worry we were trying to suppress was seeping through our calm exteriors. She might have been young but she certainly wasn't stupid. She knew her brother as well as we did. She too knew something was wrong.

'Okay,' I said, as we jumped back in the car. 'Let's go and see if the police can help us find Damien.'

It took only five minutes to drive to Cowes Police Station. As we circled the streets nearby, looking for a place to park, I heaved a sigh of relief. The rain had eased and I spotted a squad car outside the station and a uniformed police officer talking to a woman in the street.

Thank goodness.

Within minutes we'd parked and were back outside the station, but the officer and the woman seemed to have moved into the parking area behind the building. Being a small island, our police stations weren't always manned, so I prayed there'd still be other officers inside.

I walked up the steps to the heavy front door, Melissa clinging on to my hand. With my free hand, I grabbed the handle and pushed. It was locked. My heart sank. Surely there was someone inside? I knocked loudly once, then twice.

'Hello?' I shouted. I felt panic building in my chest, shortening my breath. I went back down the steps and picked up the phone that was situated outside the station. I knew it connected to the main headquarters in Newport.

'Police,' came the voice on the other end of the line.

'Hello,' I said. 'I am at Cowes Police Station. I need to speak to an officer.'

'I'm sorry, there's no one in Cowes Station at the moment,' the man said, nonchalantly.

I sucked my breath in sharply. How on earth could that be? There was a light on inside and I'd just seen an officer. Emotions churned inside me – annoyance, confusion, dismay, upset. Suddenly, another emotion began to boil up inside: frustration. I couldn't suppress it.

Someone must be in there, surely!

I started to shake as adrenaline pumped through me. I'd never felt like this before. Hot tears streamed down my face. When I spoke, I barely recognised my voice as my own.

'I need to report a missing person,' I said between sobs. 'One of my children is missing. My son.'

There was a pause. The officer had clearly been taken aback by the sudden explosion of emotion. 'One moment,' he said. 'Let me try the station again.'

The line went silent for what seemed like an eternity. My shoulders tensed and I could almost hear my heart pounding out of my chest, as Melissa and I clung to one another. Then suddenly, from behind us, came a creaking noise. I spun on my heel and saw a crack of light appearing around the station's doorframe.

Exhaling slowly, I felt some of the tension in my body dissipate. Oddly, despite the panic that must have been communicated to those inside, the door seemed to open in slow motion. Maybe it was my mind playing tricks, but there didn't seem to be any sense of urgency. We stumbled up the steps together, Melissa holding on to me tightly. As we stepped inside, I gasped. I saw not one, but a group of officers milling around the station.

Had they been ignoring my desperate knocking?

It didn't matter. I was there. Walking into the fluorescent glow of the station's reception I tried to compose myself, so I could articulate that Damien was missing. But panicked pleas spun round my head.

Help me, please help me. I need help. I can't find my son. Please help.

I was in a dreamlike state as we were taken into a room and sat down to fill in a missing person report, Melissa still clinging to me like a vine. Suddenly being where I needed to be, with people I knew could help, focused me. Sharp as a tack, I diligently answered every last question about Damien.

I told them he was only sixteen but very tall. I explained how he'd been out with his best friend and they'd only separated when they decided to go home, but that Damien had never turned up. I told them what he was wearing. I told them everything. Every last detail I could find in the corners of my brain. When I was done, I looked the officer square in the eye.

'He always lets me know where he is, you know.' I said. 'I know something is wrong.'

The officer raised an eyebrow. 'Thank you, Mrs Nettles,' he said.

'So what now?' I asked. I perched on the edge of my seat, anxiously awaiting instruction. I'd never imagined myself in this situation but, from watching the news over the years, I expected this to be the part when the machine swung into action. A missing child was always a priority, right?

'We'll put this out to our officers, to keep an eye out,' he said with a slight shrug. 'You should just go home and wait. He'll probably show up.'

'Pardon?' I said, dumbfounded. I suppose he could, but he hadn't.

That was why I was here!

'Lots of teenagers do this, especially boys,' he said. 'They're usually having some problems. A funny five minutes. They go off to sort themselves out and then turn back up. He'll be home by teatime.'

My jaw swung open as I tried to get my head around the comment. I'd just told him that my son hadn't been seen since 10:30pm the previous night. He missed his curfew and wasn't with any of his friends. I told him it was out of character.

And that was his response? *He'll be home by teatime . . .*

I took a breath. I was sure he meant well but it offered no comfort. In fact, it disturbed me that because Damien was a teenage boy they assumed he must have been off gallivanting somewhere. Run away after an argument. Having a funny five minutes, whatever the heck *that* was. I was confused.

'You know what boys are like,' another officer chipped in.

I shook my head, mouth still gaping wide. I didn't, actually. I knew what *Damien* was like. And I knew this was out of character. Yet I felt all my concerns were falling on deaf ears.

Damien was doing great at school. Of course he had his ups and downs, but nothing out of the ordinary. And our home life? Well, it was *normal*. I'd come to the police with the concern that something terrible might have happened to my son. I hadn't for one second even considered that Damien might have not come home out of choice. The idea was, quite frankly, ludicrous. Despite the clear lack of interest, I sat glued to my seat, waiting for more. Some action . . . *something*.

'Just go home and wait,' the officer said, urging me to my feet and ushering me out of the room, towards the station door. 'We'll call you as soon as we hear anything.'

I was left dumbstruck by the flippant response. Surely that wasn't it? Surely they would do more?

'Good evening, Mrs Nettles,' the officer said. Then the door shut.

Apparently not.

I barely remembered driving home. My mind was clouded by swirling thoughts. Why was there no search party? No boots on the ground? No plane in the air, scouring for signs of my boy? Why weren't they listening to me? I was telling them this was out of character. How could they ignore a mother's instinct?

The more these thoughts churned in my head, the more I began to question myself, though. Had I expected too much?

Believed too much of what I'd seen on TV? Was this really the normal process for dealing with a happy sixteen-year-old boy from a loving home who'd inexplicably just not come home?

Back home I fell into Ed's arms. 'I feel so foolish,' I sobbed. 'They treated me like I was overreacting.'

'You're not,' said Ed. 'This isn't like Damien.'

We weren't the only ones who thought so. By now news had spread that he was missing. My brother Nigel was making his way to us from Gloucestershire and, after waiting to see if he ended up in Portsmouth, Sarah had decided to head home from her student digs.

Friends and family came to the house, sharing information, scouring the streets and making endless cups of tea. None of them thought I was overreacting. But that was because they knew Damien like we did.

By now I was sure he was hurt somewhere. In my heart I believed he needed to be rescued. What other explanation could there be? I racked my brain to think of anything else we could do.

Before moving back to the Isle of Wight in 1990, we'd lived in the USA. There had been a high-profile missing person case and I remembered pictures being shared on the sides of milk cartons and on posters around towns. I was sure there was a charity or organisation behind it. There must be one in the UK too. What was it called?

'Missing Persons,' I said aloud, as I flicked through the Yellow Pages. I found the number and dialled it, hands shaking.

'Hello, Missing Persons Helpline,' a warm, gentle voice said.

'I need to report a missing person,' I replied, voice shaking. 'My son Damien didn't come home last night.'

'Okay, I'm sorry to hear that. Let me take some details,' the voice replied, filled with genuine concern. 'How old is he and how long has he been missing?'

'He's only sixteen. He was out with friends. We expected him home at midnight last night but no one seems to have seen him since half past ten,' I explained.

'Okay, I understand,' the lady said.

'I know it's not been that long,' I started to explain, 'but it's just not like him.'

'If it's out of character, it's good that you've reported it,' she reassured me. 'The first few hours are very important.'

She told me her name was Claudia and that I could call her with any new information. I was assigned a caseworker and she provided me with a checklist of things to do: call the police and make an official report. Contact family and friends.

We'd already done everything.

Although it changed nothing immediately, just hearing someone accept my concerns filled me with hope. Someone was actually hearing me; understanding what I was going through. I felt I had been lifted a little out of the black hole I was sinking into. It felt like they cared – unlike the police at our local station.

Of course I knew it was early days. By now, only twenty-four hours had passed since I had last seen Damien. Twenty-four hours since he'd pleaded with me to let him stay out until midnight. Twenty-four hours since I'd kissed him goodbye. But every second felt like a lifetime. I'd followed all of the instructions given by the police and waited. But still I'd heard nothing. Damien still hadn't 'turned back up'.

Teatime came and went. There was no phone call. No tall silhouette slinking off the bus at the stop outside our living-room window, striding up the path to get out of the rain.

No message passed on by a friend of a friend, as sometimes happened on the island.

Nothing. Just silence.

On an island where you couldn't sneeze without someone saying 'bless you', where people knew your business before you did, it was odd. I couldn't just sit around waiting, but I felt powerless. There was nothing else I could do alone. I needed the police to act. Surely something should be happening by now? A few hours after I'd reported him missing, I picked up our phone and dialled the station.

'None of this makes sense. I'm sure he must be somewhere where he can't reach help,' I said in desperation. 'Can't you get the rescue dogs out?' I'd seen them in action on the island before, so why weren't they out now?

'Mrs Nettles, the dogs would be no good,' the officer huffed. 'It's been twenty-four hours since he was last seen and it's been raining, so any scent will have washed away.'

Maybe not if you'd acted faster, I thought, fleetingly.

'Well, what about the spotter plane?' I begged.

'It's out of action, Mrs Nettles. You really are hampering our investigation with all these calls,' he snapped accusingly.

I was stung. I was a mother with a missing son. A tall, gangly, immature little boy who had only turned sixteen in the summer. I was trying to make sense of what was happening. His attitude and tone really didn't help. And as for the 'investigation', if there was one going on, then I wanted them to include me in it. Not leave me pestering from the sidelines. I needed updates; reassurance that my son's life and wellbeing was a priority. That they were 'on it'. I opened my mouth to say as much, but the officer continued to chastise me.

'Quite frankly, you are not doing yourself or your son any favours by calling up all the time,' he barked, emotionless and irate. It was like a slap across the face.

'B–but...' I stuttered, trying to find the words to communicate my anguish. Here I was, a mother desperately frightened for the son she had brought into this world, whom she'd loved and protected for sixteen years. And *I* was the problem here?

'Unless you have anything to report, Mrs Nettles, we have no further news,' the officer said. 'Leave us to do our job.' As the line clicked dead I stood frozen, suspended in disbelief.

Was this real?

Anger welled up inside me. I could barely believe the conversations I was having.

Damien had been here just a few hours ago. Saturday had been a normal day like any other. We'd been shopping in Newport as a family. We'd picked up Damien's new school trousers and he wanted to spend a gift voucher he'd received for doing well in his GCSEs. He loved music, and played the guitar and the trombone. He was even in a band with some friends. While we were out he'd bought a book about guitars, along with some new strings for his instrument. After that I'd left the boys and Melissa with Ed while I went to have my hair done. It was a rare treat and something I didn't do often enough, having four kids and a husband that worked away all week.

Other than our shopping trip, though, he hadn't planned much for the weekend. He'd mentioned his ex-girlfriend, Abbie Mabey, might pop round on Sunday, but even that wasn't firm, as he'd told me he had lots of studying to do. He'd recently decided he wanted to be a marine biologist and the realisation of the grades he needed to get at A Level had suddenly kicked in.

He'd started really taking responsibility for his schoolwork and I'd been so proud of his commitment. He'd even helped Sarah study for her Psychology A Level, developing a keen interest in the subject as a result. His decision to go out with Chris and Davey had been a spur of the moment thing, and I'd agreed. I knew the family well and the boys had been firm friends for a long time. What reason did I have to stop him?

There was nothing unusual about anything that happened that day. Nothing at all.

But where was he now? The juxtaposition of the complete normality of the previous day to the moment I was now in led my mind astray. Nightmarish visions filled my head once again. Had he walked along the seafront and fallen into the sea? Was he lying in a ditch somewhere? Had he been hit by a car?

Panic rose inside of me with every new imagined scenario. I felt a slow welling up of emotion, an ache in my core that made me feel I was about to explode. I didn't want to distress the children, so I started to climb the stairs to our bedroom. There was a gentle hum of conversation punctuated by the occasional clink of teacups, but trapped in the bubble of anguish I could barely hear anything. I dragged myself along the landing towards the bedroom, biting my lip to stifle the sobs that pushed against my lips. It was only when the bedroom door clicked shut behind me that I finally allowed the enormity of our situation to sink in.

I collapsed into a heap on the bed, like a dead weight. Then I opened my mouth and it came. It wasn't a cry, or a sob. It wasn't even a gut wrench. It came from deep down in my soul, where the bonds with all my children lay. It was a sound so primal, so guttural, it defied description. A sound of such deep and uncontrollable anguish that it terrified me. The sound of a mother helpless to save her child from danger.

The tears started to fall hot and fast over my cheeks, my whole body heaving with emotion as I asked the same unanswered questions over and again in my head.

Where was he? Where was my Damien?

CHAPTER THREE

I DON'T KNOW HOW LONG I CRIED FOR BUT EVENTUALLY EXHAUSTION overwhelmed me, physically at least. The house fell silent and Ed slipped into our bed. He'd remained dignified, calm and composed all day, keeping us all positive and focused. But now, in the private sanctuary of our bedroom, he finally broke down. Like me, every fear he'd pushed down and every emotion he'd stifled came flooding out. Uncontrollable tears streaked his face, his cries coming from deep in his core.

Ed was an eternal optimist. I'd never seen him like this, so broken. Every sob felt like a dagger to my already aching heart. What's more, his deep distress signalled to me that he felt the same sense of foreboding. Both of us knew we should get some rest, but we were too stricken with fear and worry to sleep. All we could do was hold one another, eyes open and minds racing. With Damien still out there somewhere, I couldn't stop running through every possible scenario.

Despite what my gut was telling me. Despite our completely

run-of-the-mill Saturday. Despite my firm belief that there had been nothing troubling Damien as he walked out of the house to see his friends, the comments the police had made earlier in the day turned over in my head: *they're usually having some problems. Go off to sort themselves out.* Was there *anything* that might have been bothering Damien? I couldn't think of anything, but I started to weigh up where I could have missed something.

In September he'd moved schools from Cowes High School to Carisbrooke High School, as Cowes didn't offer Psychology as an A Level. He'd being enjoying his new courses and he knew a handful of people who had also transferred from his old school, but he hadn't quite settled in yet. I'd been anxious for him, but he seemed to be dealing with it in his own way, taking opportunities to mix and socialise with the kids from his new school. It was early days and he seemed okay. So if that wasn't it, was there something else I might have missed? Something he felt he needed to sort out?

I thought hard and cast my mind as far back as I could. We were an ordinary family, but to others I suppose our lives could have seemed quite extraordinary. For starters, our family was half-American – something fairly exotic for the island. I'd lived all over England as a child, moving with my father's job, but spent much of my young life on the Isle of Wight. Then, when I was fifteen, we all moved over to the USA.

I'd met Ed in New Orleans, when I'd been living and studying in the States. He was a handsome Louisianan who'd recently left Greece, where he'd been stationed with the American Air Force. It was 1975. He was bright and gregarious. I was a flower child determined to be part of a generation that would make a change. We were both hungry to see more of the world, so we did – even as we started our own family, with Sarah arriving first in 1977. At such a young age we believed that experiencing different cultures and countries would be more likely to enhance their lives than harm them.

After getting married we moved all over the world with Ed's job as an international sales manager, from cities across the USA and UK to Singapore, where Damien was born.

Tears pricked my eyes as I remembered the day he arrived. It was 1:27am on 21 June 1980 at Gleneagles Hospital in Singapore.

'It's a . . . it's a . . . IT'S A BOY!' Ed had exclaimed, fizzing over with joy as our first born son burst into the world.

As the nurse placed the 7lb 10oz scrap in my arms, I fell deeply in love with my first baby boy. Two big brown eyes stared up at me and I swear I felt my heart burst. He had long legs and long fingers that curled tightly around mine.

'He's going to be tall!' said the doctor with a smile. Ed and I looked at each other lovingly, then back to our new baby boy.

'Hello, Damien,' I whispered gently in his ear, kissing his forehead as I nuzzled him closer.

Having our baby boy was one miracle, but in the days that followed another happened.

When I'd had Sarah I'd not been able to feed her myself and, despite having an abundance of support from Ed and both of our families, I'd felt like a complete failure. But with Damien it just happened. I'd been filled with maternal pride and an overwhelming bond with the tiny human that was nestled into my chest. An unbreakable connection.

I'll always protect you, no matter what, I promised silently, as he gazed up at me. Our hearts were full and our lives were nothing short of perfect.

In 1984 James arrived, followed by Melissa in 1987, completing our brood. The years that followed put some challenges in our way. Ed's job and changes in the economy meant we had to move even more frequently. Eventually we ended up on the Isle of Wight, where I'd grown up. Ed got a job in London, living on the outskirts of the city in the week and returning to the island at the weekend. I looked after the children and later began studying for my NVQ in IT and Office Administration.

We made our home in the village of Gurnard, overlooking the Solent, where my brother Nigel and I had lived and attended school as children. My parents had also moved back a few years earlier, so it felt a lot like going home. My own memories of growing up on 'the garden isle' were filled with endless summers playing on the beach and enjoying walks across fields and cliffs with our parents. I wanted that for my family too.

Truth be told, I worried about all of my children, and America didn't always feel safe enough for my liking. There were daily shootings and crime-related deaths. I didn't want my kids to grow up immune to the horror of these things, to accept it as normal. I wanted them to have the simpler, quieter life that I'd had growing up. The island was minute in comparison to the sprawling American towns we'd called home, and it felt much safer too. We were finally laying down some solid roots. Just in time for Sarah starting secondary school, with Damien not far behind.

There had been changes since I'd last lived on the island, of course. We moved back in 1990, when Damien was ten, and the island was noticeably more cosmopolitan and vibrant. The annual Cowes Week regatta still attracted wealthy 'yachties' each year and there were now droves of educated and diverse 'overners' – people from the mainland who'd chosen to move to the island to escape the crammed cities of the south coast and beyond.

On the flipside to that, the Isle of Wight had also long been home to three prisons, and many of the families of convicts housed in HMPs Albany, Camp Hill and Parkhurst had also made their home on the island. I guess they'd been there when I was a kid but I'd never really noticed. As an adult with a young family, you saw things a little differently.

Some were locals, others came from further afield, but you could always pick them out. They were the ones who were always in the pubs, flogging something that had 'just fallen off the back of a lorry', or who knew someone who could get a TV or radio at a too-good-to-be true price. Nothing was ever quite kosher. They were easy enough to avoid, though.

The one thing that had definitely remained constant from my youth, however, was the 'them and us' mentality. Most of the native islanders were friendly enough, but we were 'overners'. We'd never be 'caulkheads' like them. They'd been born there and we hadn't. Simple as that. It was an invisible divide that had prevailed through the decades.

Despite my motherly worries, and aside from the odd jibe about having 'phoney American accents', nothing about the move seemed to affect Damien or his brother and sisters. They were close to one another and each made their own friends. They were resilient and had taken it all in their stride. Or so I'd thought. But *had* I missed anything?

Suddenly my meandering thoughts ground to a halt. A memory flashed into my mind.

There *had* been one incident, a few weeks earlier, soon after

Damien had started his new school. In the chaos of the past few hours it had completely slipped my mind, almost insignificant in the panic surrounding his disappearance.

Damien had asked if he could go to a house party on the other side of the island with a group of kids from his new school. I was pleased to hear he was making friends but reluctant to let him stay overnight at the home of a complete stranger.

'I'm not sure,' I'd said, anxiously.

'Please, Mum,' he'd said. 'You know I don't have many friends at school. This is my chance to meet them and feel like one of the crowd.'

How could I deny him that? 'Okay,' I'd said. 'Just be careful. If anything happened to you, I would just die.'

'Of course I will, Mum,' he'd beamed.

The day after the party he'd called me to collect him from an affluent area not far from Yafford Mill, a hamlet about six miles south-west of Newport. When I'd arrived he was already outside waiting.

'Did you have a good night?' I asked, as he climbed into the car.

'It was the most humiliating night of my life, Mum,' he said, looking at me.

'Why, what happened?' I asked, as we drove off.

The whole story came tumbling out. There had been booze at the party. The kids got drunk and silly and picked on him because he was the new boy. They'd drawn on him with a marker, scorched his jacket and even shot a pellet gun at his head. I pulled the car over abruptly.

'Damien, that's assault,' I said. 'You can't let them get away with that. We're going back now to sort it out, or I'm calling the police.'

'Mum, NO!' he said.

I sucked in a breath and bit my tongue. I could understand how difficult this was for him. Things were tough enough being the new kid and I didn't want to add to his insult.

'It was a joke that got out of hand because people were drunk,' he continued after a moment. 'I don't want to make a big issue out of it.'

'Are you sure?' I asked, one last time.

'Yes,' he said firmly. 'Just leave it.'

To me it seemed wrong to let those horrible kids get away with what they'd done.

The fact that it had even happened in the first place made me worry too. There was something about Damien that just felt more vulnerable than his siblings. He had such a sweet, trusting nature and could be a little gullible at times. I'd never been able to put my finger on it, but I'd always had a greater sense of fear for him than for his siblings.

The weekend passed and I could tell he was nervous about going back to school, but he didn't make a fuss. Monday came and went and, as far as I knew, nothing else was ever said about the incident. But now, how could I be sure?

As the memory flooded back I felt the urge to leap out of bed and call the police, tell them what I'd recalled in case it helped at all, but something stopped me. I didn't want to do anything that would allow them to brush me off as hysterical. I needed to keep them on my side. Besides, these were brand-new 'friends'. I didn't know their names or where they lived. With Damien not at home to ask, where would I even begin? All I could do for now was make a mental note of the story and try to force myself to sleep.

The following day, the police remained silent and, to my heavy eyes, inactive. Instead, it was our family and friends who galvanised and took immediate action. Damien's friends' parents took time out to come and sit with me and try to come up with something that might lead us to him. Posters and flyers with his beaming face had been made by Chris Boon's family in their little copy shop, and friends had plastered them all over the island with the bold headline: MISSING. Between friends, family and people we each knew, we pieced together what we could of Damien's movements on the night he'd disappeared.

We'd learned that he and Chris had left the party in East Cowes at 9:15pm. The guests had been Chris's little brother Davey and some girls he knew. It was a younger crowd, so they'd got bored. After leaving the party they headed to the local Alldays shop, where Damien bought some bottles of cider.

'I wonder where he got the money for the cider,' I said to Ed. 'He only took a few pounds out with him.'

They then caught a small boat called the *Jenny Lee* to Cowes at 9:45pm. They'd wandered around town for approximately half an hour, seeing who was out and about. Then they'd begun their walk home.

So far, so normal.

The boys parted ways at 10:30pm by Granville Road, not far from Northwood Park. What happened next was still unclear. We had eyes and ears everywhere, yet none of them seemed to belong to the police. The only real contact we'd had from them was a few phone calls and a couple of visits to our house by random uniformed police officers carrying scraps of wet clothing in plastic bags, asking if we recognised them as Damien's, but we never did.

Frustrated that there had been no official search party, Ed, James and my father, Jack, took matters into their own hands. They pulled on their coats and battled against the elements to search the seafront between Gurnard and Cowes and the shortcuts through the Solent School fields that could only be accessed through swathes of thick matted bushes. We knew local kids often used these routes to get home quicker, so it was worth a try.

If only the police were out there.

Instead, a twelve-year-old boy, a man in his seventies and my husband were out there alone in the dark, wind and rain, armed only with torches, shouting Damien's name as they scrambled over barbed wire and crawled through undergrowth – hoping against hope to hear his voice call back. It was ludicrous. I couldn't help but voice my despair while visiting the home of Damien's friend, Jeff Laurens.

'I just don't understand it,' I said to Jeff's mum, Corran. 'Why aren't the police doing more?'

Corran placed a hand on my arm. 'Valerie,' she said earnestly. 'Listen to me. Don't waste your time with the police here. They won't do anything. Get out there yourself. Bang on shop doors. Do whatever it takes, but don't wait for them.'

I was taken aback. Corran was a well-respected woman, a history professor and town councillor. To hear this opinion of the police from her was completely unexpected. I didn't want to pry, but from what little she revealed it appeared she had some knowledge of the local force, and some experiences that hadn't met her expectations. It was exactly how I'd felt from the moment I'd reported Damien missing.

Over the course of a week, every call I made or request for

help was met with inaction. I heard along the grapevine that the police had been in touch with our local paper, the *Isle of Wight County Press*, asking them to print an appeal to ask people to check their sheds and outbuildings to see if Damien was there. But if they were doing anything else, they weren't telling me. Time after time they dismissed me and my support network as a bunch of hysterical mothers. They even said as much to Corran's face. I couldn't understand it. Why did they expect me to be anything else when my child was missing?

Eventually I found out. Steeled by Corran's advice I shared all the details we'd gathered of Damien's movements on the night he'd disappeared with the police and asked if they could make a reconstruction for the television news. *That's how you jog people's memories, right? That's what the police do to help find missing people?*

I was told my request had to be sent up the chain, out of the island force's hands and over to the top brass in Hampshire Constabulary. I'd been waiting at home for the call back when I saw a surly police officer I recognised as PC Nigel Williams, in full uniform, making his way up our front path, head slightly bowed against the wind.

My heart leapt into my mouth. It was ten o'clock at night. My previous requests had been responded to by a phone call, usually by an officer we'd never had contact with before. Ed and I exchanged a panicked glance. *Could this mean . . .*

We didn't say a word to one another. The panic in our eyes said it all as we both rose to our feet, even before the doorbell rang. *Please, no*, I prayed. Fear tightened vice-like around my throat, as I lurched towards the door. I could hardly breathe.

'Yes?' I whispered, as I opened the door. It was all I could manage as I prepared to hear the news that every parent dreads. My body was already beginning to shake.

'I just wanted to come and tell you that there won't be any reconstruction of your son's footsteps,' he said, matter-of-factly.

'What?' I exclaimed, turning to Ed in disbelief. I felt like I'd been punched in the stomach. *Was that it?*

My head began to spin as PC Williams began reeling off the intricacies, so much so that I only caught snippets of his little 'update'. After a few seconds, though, I snapped back into the room and held a hand out to stop the tirade of noise pouring from his lips.

'Why have you come to my house at 10pm just to tell us that?' I said, my blood boiling. 'Why couldn't you have just come tomorrow?'

Did they even have the first clue about what we were going through? What the sight of a uniformed officer on our doorstep late at night could possibly mean to us?

The officer looked at me like I was stark raving mad. 'I just thought you would like to know,' he snapped brusquely. 'Anyway, Mrs Nettles, your son is nineteen, so he can do what he wants.'

Nineteen? My mouth fell open. Ed's did too. *Did he just say nineteen?*

'Pardon?' I asked. I had to be sure I'd heard correctly.

'I said he's nineteen. An adult. He can do what he wants,' he repeated.

Panic rose in my chest and my body began shaking again. 'No. No. He's not. He's sixteen,' I said, horrified. I could hear my voice rising. 'He turned sixteen in June,' I continued, reiterating my point. 'Where did you get nineteen from?'

I couldn't quite remember, but I thought Officer Williams

had been at the station the night I'd reported Damien missing. Surely he'd remember a mother coming in to report a missing sixteen-year-old?

Stunned, he stared at me for a moment. 'It was in your report. . .' he said, trailing off, as if he was unsure where the information had come from.

'I said he was sixteen. Where did you get nineteen from?' I repeated, incredulous. I'd noted down Damien's birthday as 21 June 1980 in that report. It was now 1996.

How could they have got such a vital piece of information so wrong? I knew there was a huge difference between the action taken when an adult goes missing and when a child vanishes. Had they been treating Damien's as an adult missing person case?

I'd always thought the British police were a cut above the rest. They found the bad guys, they helped the good guys, they did the right thing and they did it well. It turned out I was wrong; they couldn't even do simple maths.

The realisation hit me like a ton of bricks. Corran's warning about the island police echoed in my head: 'Don't waste your time with the police here.' She couldn't have been more right. Either they didn't care or didn't know what they were doing. Whatever it was, I knew in that moment we were on our own. We'd co-operate with the police, of course. Tell them everything we discovered. But we'd have to find Damien ourselves.

CHAPTER FOUR

A LMOST A WEEK HAD PASSED SINCE DAMIEN HAD LAST BEEN SEEN. Our home became a hub of activity, an incident room where Damien's friends and their parents would come to share any news or ideas they might have about his whereabouts. And seek a little solace. People just felt like they needed to be there.

After realising the failings of the police, I'd immediately heeded Corran's advice and taken matters into my own hands. Anything I believed the police should be doing I decided to do myself. I wasn't short of resources.

On any given day, at any given time, there might be ten people, maybe more, packed into our small living room. It was a mish-mash of mid-90s decor. Pale, pink-tinged wallpaper and flowery curtains provided the backdrop to a plush blue couch with an ornate white pattern and a matching armchair that Damien loved to sprawl on after school.

There'd be even more people crammed in our long galley

37

kitchen, providing a steady stream of tea and biscuits. Chris Boon would be there, of course, along with Abbie and her new boyfriend Neil. There was our daughter Sarah and her friend Karen and countless others, not to mention the kids' parents, when they weren't working.

Every single one of us was completely baffled.

There would be long periods of silence as we analysed even our most basic conversations with Damien. We worked through possible scenarios that may have played out on that night and strained to think of places he may have gone to. From time to time, suggestions would be made. Ideas all tossed into the ring for further debate, but none led to a solid conclusion.

In the absence of any answers, or any official police action, we decided to mount our own mass search of the island – a week to the day since Damien had last been seen. Ahead of the search we printed more posters and plastered them all over Cowes and Newport. They may only have been black-and-white handouts, but they wildly outnumbered the Hampshire Constabulary appeal posters that appeared suddenly in the wake of my conversation about Damien's age.

In fact, outside of our own posters, the only one that really stuck in my mind was a big display poster that the National Missing Persons Helpline had created. It featured the faces of lots and lots of missing people. Despite all my anguish, when I saw it, it made me smile. There, next to Damien's beaming face, was the face of Richey Edwards, the guitarist from the Manic Street Preachers, who had disappeared at the start of 1995.

I wish Damien could see this, I thought. He was a huge fan of the Manics. He was a guitarist too, so he was essentially in the same gallery as one of his idols. If only it was in a different hall of fame, I thought sadly, as the lightness of the moment left me. Instead, like Richey, his face was accompanied by a stark and impersonal description.

Missing: Damien Nettles
- *White*
- *Six foot three inches tall*
- *Slim build*
- *Short brown hair, shaved at the back*
- *Brown eyes*

Last seen wearing:
- *Black fleece jacket with grey collar*
- *Dark-blue jeans*
- *Black boots*

It was painful seeing my son's entire being reduced to eight bullet points on a side of A4 paper. He was so much more than just that.

Hampshire Constabulary's attempts to make up lost time seemed half-hearted, and I certainly didn't feel the force's attitude towards me had changed at all, despite now knowing Damien was a child. I didn't even so much as receive an apology from them for getting his age wrong. They continued to dismiss any suggestions I offered up about his disappearance, too.

'What about paedophiles?' I asked. After reading an article in the local paper, I'd learned that recently released sex offenders were being placed in halfway houses all over the island.

'On no, Mrs Nettles,' one officer said flippantly. 'Your son would be too tall and too old for them.' Maybe so, but how could they dismiss the idea outright?

Perhaps they'd already looked into it?

We still had the occasional police officer turning up unannounced on the doorstep, openly clutching rags in evidence bags, asking me if I recognised them as Damien's. Couldn't they understand how traumatic that was? Didn't they care? Every time an officer arrived I would start to shake and struggle to breathe. Every time it happened I was expecting the worst.

* * *

The day of the search arrived. I'd stayed at home as I was still frightened that Damien might come back and I would miss him. In the living room I flicked on the TV and turned to the local BBC news. It was a habit I'd long had, but since Damien had vanished it was now filled with trepidation. You see, the island was no stranger to bodies washing up on shore or people falling from the cliffs. Stories like that made the headlines all the time.

Maybe it sounds a little heartless, but if there was no one you were worried about, it was background noise. But not now. Now I waited for those stories. I didn't want our search for Damien to end like that. I caught the report just as it was broadcasting what appeared to be scenes from Cowes town centre. The screen was filled with faces I recognised. Suddenly I realised: it was Damien's friends and their families.

It was our search party.

There they were, pacing the streets searching for clues, poking in and out of alleys and local shortcuts, calling out my boy's name. Doing exactly what I'd expected the police to do the first day that Damien hadn't come home.

A full-scale search party. Media on site.

An earnest-looking reporter appeared on screen and spoke as a picture of Damien popped up. My heart leapt. Finally. People were taking notice. We'd had good support from the island's weekly local paper, the *Isle of Wight County Press*. I'd spoken to a reporter and, the Friday after Damien had disappeared, they published a story and our appeal for information. But this was the first time the story had made TV news.

A wave of vindication washed over me. If it was enough to make the regional TV news, none of my emotions had been in any way an overreaction. It *was* serious. Not just a 'funny five minutes'. I had no idea how the local media had found out about the search. Perhaps they'd seen our posters, or maybe it had been word of mouth. To be honest I didn't care. I was just glad it was happening.

The story was covered all over the region, reaching people in the county and beyond, in Southampton, Portsmouth and even as far as Kent. Hundreds of thousands of people would now be aware that Damien was missing and be seeing his image far and wide. There would be more eyes and ears to watch out for him. I knew this was now bigger than our small island home.

Eyes still fixed firmly on the TV report I spotted something in the background. Poking a long stick aimlessly in a bush and looking almost lost among the crowds were two uniformed police officers. I laughed incredulously. Now the cameras were on, they'd decided to turn up.

Where had they been last week?

I didn't have time to dwell on my anger, though; with the

eyes of the media now trained on us, there was much more to do. After scouring Cowes town centre, the search party took to Northwood Park – not far from where Chris had last seen Damien – and paced slowly but steadily through the graveyard towards St Mary's Church.

Nearby, another group moved through an overgrown network of passages under Northwood Park. I'd never been there, but I knew they were known locally as 'the tunnels', and kids on the island loved to hang out and play there. A few miles away, a prison service dog handler, who happened to be a friend of a friend, had taken his own prison-service dog along to try and pick up any trace of Damien's presence in the woods.

Around forty people had turned up to help that day, searching for hours until they lost the light. There was genuine concern for Damien and the community had mobilised. The outpouring of love and support brought me comfort. The attention of the media further steeled my resolve. But there was still no sign of my son. Every time our phone rang, I hoped it would be him. I was convinced he was somewhere on the island. After all, he couldn't just disappear.

I continued to heed Corran's advice and pushed on with my own detective work, taking to the streets and joining friends to knock on the doors of the pubs and shops around town that would have been open the night that Damien was last seen. A few people, including Sarah's friend Karen, said they had seen Damien in town earlier in the evening. She'd said hello, asked if he was okay and given him a hug, before they'd gone their separate ways.

Just like they had on many a Saturday night over the years.

It was sightings like this that put Damien in specific places. Places that allowed us to focus our 'unofficial' investigation on key areas. As we pounded the pavement, showing Damien's photo and asking question after question of friends, acquaintances and strangers, a fuller picture of that night began to emerge. People confirmed seeing Damien at the Duke of York pub at around ten o'clock, shortly before a worker from the local chip shop, Yorkies, remembered seeing him too. He said he'd come into the shop, picked up a salt cellar and waved it in the air, shouting, 'All right.' Apparently he didn't buy anything; he'd just popped in and out again.

As various accounts revealed how he and Chris had steadily made their way into town, Damien had been seen going in and out of pubs, apparently looking for his sister. A number of people told us that he'd said she was coming back from the mainland and didn't want to miss seeing her.

'Did you make any plans?' I asked her.

'We did mention it,' Sarah confirmed. 'But we didn't set anything in stone.'

In the end she stayed in Portsmouth, but she didn't explicitly tell Damien that she wasn't coming. He didn't know. Which supported what people were saying.

He'd been spotted hovering outside a local gaming place called The Arcade, and had then been outside The Fountain, trying to get into that pub too. Oddly, he was eating chips at the time. The licensee had even turned him away until he finished eating them. But they couldn't have been from Yorkies.

'Maybe he got them at the other chip shop?' I said to Ed.

'Where else would they have come from?' he agreed. But there was nothing to confirm it.

We knew that Damien and Chris had parted ways not long after that. Chris thought that Damien was going to walk through Northwood Park to get home, but accounts from a few other witnesses revealed that he'd actually turned around and walked back into town.

But why? To keep looking for Sarah?

With all this information on board, we returned to each location armed with posters. We asked again and again: 'Did you see Damien?'

Finally, we had a breakthrough.

Corran spoke to the owner of Yorkies chip shop and he casually mentioned that the shop had CCTV. He told her he'd be more than happy to hand the tape over to us immediately. Corran called me and, shortly afterwards, we went to the chip shop to speak to staff and collect the tape. As we were waiting, the manageress appeared from behind the counter and joined us.

'I saw Damien that night, you know,' she said. 'In the shop.'

'Did you serve him?' I asked, keen to glean any new information from her.

'No, one of the lads did,' she said. 'But I saw him. He was the last customer to leave before I locked up.'

'How did he seem?' Corran asked.

'He seemed a bit wobbly.' Then she laughed. 'The guy who served him couldn't hear him when he was ordering, and they went back and forth for a while.'

'Did you notice anything else?' I pushed. The smile fell from her lips.

'He didn't smell of alcohol or anything,' she said, seriously. 'But maybe he was on something?'

'On something?' I asked.

'Drugs,' she said. 'A lot of them that come in here are.'

I frowned. We *knew* Damien had been drinking, so it seemed strange that she couldn't smell it on him. I also couldn't help but feel she was being very quick to judge. But I decided to bite my lip until I'd seen the footage.

The owner eventually appeared and handed the tape to us. After leaving the chip shop we walked through town, ending up in Northwood Park at the church. We decided to go inside to say a prayer. Choir practice was taking place and a few people were dotted around the pews. Corran and I silently sat down. As the music rang in my ears, the enormity of the situation we were in hit me all at once.

Damien was missing and I was scared. *Terrified.* I burst into racking sobs, my whole body heaving. People turned to look, somewhat startled by the outburst. I was embarrassed, but I couldn't hold it back.

'Oh, Val,' Corran said, leaning in to comfort me. But I was inconsolable. The thought had been lingering in the back of my mind, but now it was front and centre – Damien wasn't going to 'just turn up'. This was serious and it was out of my control.

Eventually I managed to compose myself. I had to. We had a new lead and action to take. Straight after we left the church I returned home and contacted the police to alert them to the videotape from Yorkies. Despite their lack of support we'd kept them up-to-date with every scrap of information we unearthed. We were doing their job for them, really. It was our way of letting them know that we weren't going to go away until they had taken note.

Until we found Damien.

The tape seemed to do the trick. The officer from Hampshire Constabulary asked me to meet him and arrange for a copy of the tape to be made. I was desperate to sit down and see what the tape had to show, but I also wanted to make sure the police had every scrap of evidence at their disposal. Dutifully, I went into town and met an officer in the doorway of some flats on Cowes High Street. I knew Sarah's friend Scott Bradley lived there. He worked at the local Blockbuster video store and had all the equipment needed to make VHS copies, so the police must've turned up and asked him to make a copy. After a few minutes the officer reappeared, handed me a VHS tape and sent me on my way.

Back at home, Ed and I gathered around our television set to watch the video. When we pressed play, the screen lit up. We paused for a minute then both of us laughed out loud. Rather than the grainy image of a chip shop CCTV camera, we were met with the opening scenes of the *Super Mario Brothers* film. Scott must have been so startled by having police officers turn up at his door that he'd taped right over the film he'd been watching. We chuckled, as we had to fast-forward through a good five minutes of the film before we reached the CCTV footage.

If Damien was here, he'd be laughing his socks off, I thought. But once the footage started rolling we fell silent. We scanned every corner of the screen as a steady stream of revellers flowed in and out of Yorkies, snaffling their late-night snacks. At one point we even spotted a police car drive past the glass window of the chip shop.

Then suddenly ... *BINGO!*

'There he is!' I exclaimed.

Smiling and towering above the six other men in the shop, as loud music played over the hubbub of conversation, Damien even appeared to engage in friendly conversation with a few of them. He looked older than his sixteen years, but it was unmistakably Damien. I grabbed Ed's hand as we watched the footage.

There he was. My boy.

I was instantly overwhelmed with love. Then frustration and anguish washed over me. Tears ran down my cheeks. He was there, right in front of me. I wanted to reach out to him, touch him, hug him.

But I couldn't.

True to witness reports that Damien had seemed 'slightly drunk', he *did* appear tipsy. A little wobbly even. But he certainly wasn't rolling drunk. I also spotted the manageress in the shot and recalled her comments about him not smelling of alcohol. Truth be told, I was annoyed. There was a counter and a vat of boiling fishy fat between her and Damien.

How could she possibly know if he smelled of alcohol or not?

As we continued to watch the video, I decided to file her comments away under 'supposition'. When it was Damien's turn to order, we leaned in closely to listen, straining to hear over the shop music. Both of us were perplexed as the scene unfolded.

'One . . . er . . . please,' Damien appeared to say to the man behind the counter.

'One?' the man replied, leaning forwards as if he couldn't quite hear him.

'Please,' Damien repeated politely, counting out change in the palm of his hand. 'One . . . one,' he repeated, glancing up slightly. Looking at the menu board behind the server's head, I realised.

'Mate, I can't hear you,' the shopkeeper replied. Well, the music was quite loud.

'Can I have one, please?' Damien replied, a little louder.

'One what?' said the shopkeeper, clearly baffled by the conversation.

'One, please,' Damien again repeated, loudly and slowly. He was being polite. Like a child expected to be nice and say 'please'.

'Do you want chips?' the shopkeeper asked, no doubt hoping to speed up the order.

'Yes,' said Damien.

He didn't seem drunk enough to be forgetting words. He was calm, polite and pleasant and there wasn't an ounce of aggravation in the exchange. But there was no denying his behaviour was a little odd. Maybe he had drunk more than his demeanour suggested?

Or was it a case of crossed wires? We'd been to Yorkies many times and I knew that item number one on the menu board was fish and chips. Had Damien been trying to order a 'number one' and given in when the conversation went around in circles?

The footage ran on and showed the man wrapping his chips while Damien waited, occasionally looking out of the door on to the street. Was he looking for someone, at someone, or just waiting? Then he collected his chips and left, disappearing into the night.

So now we knew at least one place Damien went after leaving Chris. But the discovery begged more unanswered questions.

Who were the men in the queue with Damien?

Why did he seem to raise his hand in greeting towards one of them?

Had they met earlier in the night?

Did they notice anything strange?

Where did Damien go after he left the chip shop?

What's more, the time and date on the footage confused me. It said 12:35am, 03NOV96 – the small hours of Sunday morning. What had he been doing for two hours after leaving Chris? It was a busy town centre on a Saturday night. There had to be a way to work it out. Then it came to me.

'There are security cameras on the High Street,' I said to Ed.

'Yes,' he replied. 'I bet he's on that footage!'

I called the police station to share the news, detailed everything we'd noted about Damien's interaction in Yorkies, and highlighted the men in the queue as potential witnesses, so they could identify and contact them. Then, once again, I appealed for help.

'Can you help us get access to the CCTV footage of the High Street from that night?' I asked. 'We're sure he'll show up on it.' With all the evidence we'd gathered ourselves, surely now they could see we had something worth following up?

'Mrs Nettles,' the officer said. 'Have you *any* idea how long it would take an officer to look at all of the footage from eight street cameras?' His tone was unpleasant and condescending.

'I'm sorry, no, I don't,' I said calmly. 'But I assumed it would be part of your job to do it.' Was it really such an extraordinary ask?

The officer continued in a disdainful tone. 'It would be impossible to do and we certainly don't have the manpower,' he said.

Impossible? I couldn't comment on manpower, but I knew that was a lie. It wasn't 'impossible'. They just didn't seem to *want* to do it. But why? Why did they have such little interest in trying to find Damien? It made no sense at all.

In the days that passed, I pushed to have the CCTV from those eight cameras examined. There was no way Ed and I or any of our supporters were backing down. We knew the information they held could be vital. Finally, they agreed to take us to the Marina, where we could view the footage. It turned out that the tapes only worked in their special VCR machines.

Ed, my sister Sally and I met an officer, Sergeant Martin Goodall, at Cowes Police Station. As we walked down Birmingham Road towards the Marina, Sergeant Goodall launched into a rant about the town's CCTV cameras.

'They're useless,' he said. 'We told the council not to get colour. It's too grainy, we can't do anything with it.' Ed and I glanced at one another. To us, the CCTV was a positive opportunity, grainy or not. Why were they instantly trying to lower our expectations?

When we arrived at the Marina we were ushered into the surveillance room and told they had found footage of Damien. Exactly as we'd expected. My heart began to race in anticipation. The room was poky and devoid of natural light and an officer was sitting quietly making notes. Alongside the video machines and monitors, I noticed some pages from a foolscap notebook that appeared to document Damien's movements. Just the sight of it caused my stomach to churn. It was a strange, heady mix of fear and excitement for what was about to be revealed. The three of us shoehorned ourselves into the tiny room with the officers and crowded around the screens. My heart was pounding as an image appeared.

'And . . . here he is,' the officer said with a flourish, as if he was unveiling a masterpiece that was the result of his hard work rather than ours. I let it pass. I was more focused on finding out what the footage could tell us. We leaned in closer and examined the grainy figure on the screen. I immediately threw my arms up in the air.

'That's not Damien,' I said, glaring at the officer. 'That's not my son.'

'Are you sure?' he said, the colour draining from his cheeks. The deadly look I shot him gave him my answer. Of course I was sure! The figure they'd selected was shorter and stockier than Damien and wearing a brown jacket and what looked like some sort of cap. Their own appeal had clearly stated he was six foot three and wearing a black fleece with a grey collar. How could they have possibly thought it was the same person? Once again, despite everything we'd put on a platter for them, Hampshire Constabulary had failed us.

Once again, we'd have to do the work ourselves.

CHAPTER FIVE

WE SPENT TWO HOURS GOING THROUGH A SELECTION OF TAPES all over again. All of them focused around the time he was seen in Yorkies, rather than earlier in the evening. It was different to the chip shop footage – a series of stills that rotated 360 degrees rather than video – but it was no less painstaking to examine.

Town had been unusually busy that night. There had been a friendly football match between a local island club and a team from the mainland. It had been a home game for the island team, so there were lots of away fans milling around. The police said they'd had a lot of officers in town that night to make sure they all got the last boat home.

They were strangers. People that weren't from our small community. Could one of them have played a role in Damien's disappearance? I wondered. It was worth considering. But first we had to pinpoint Damien's whereabouts. It was like trying to find a needle in a haystack. Several tapes in, we still hadn't seen him. As we trawled through the footage from a camera that had been fixed to a wall in the High Street, a few feet from the bottom of Sun Hill, I steeled myself for disappointment.

The pubs had emptied out at around 11:30pm and the town had been heaving with activity. The narrow, grey-paved High Street was packed with revellers chatting to friends, waiting for cabs or swaying drunkenly around. Within minutes they were all but gone – scattered like startled cockroaches, scurrying up side streets. If we were going to see Damien, surely we would have done so by now? Then, at around 11:50pm, I spotted something: a gangly figure coming into view, holding something in his hands. *A portion of chips!*

'There he is!' I exclaimed. Ambling along the street in the direction of a local bus stop, it was Damien. He wandered past the camera and out of view until, a few minutes later, at around 12:02am, he reappeared, chips still in hand. He didn't look particularly drunk. In fact, he strode along in a straight line, looking calm and at ease.

Like he didn't have a care in the world. Like he was heading home.

Adrenaline surged through my body. Conflicting emotions overwhelmed me. I was excited, happy even. But it didn't stop the tears from falling. I yearned to reach out to him. Just like with the footage from Yorkies, it felt like he was in front of me, so close. Yet too far away for me to help him.

'We need to look at the other footage,' I said. 'We need to work out where else he'd been.' And where he went next. But we were forced to call it a night.

* * *

When we got home I could barely sleep. Over the course of a few days I'd been bombarded with so many fragments of information. Shards of a story that hadn't quite unfolded. We'd managed to work out that the clock on the camera in Yorkies hadn't been set back for the seasonal adjustment, so Damien had in fact been there at 11:35pm. But even with that straight, it was still so confusing and nothing threw me more than the conflicting reports about his general demeanour.

Most people who had seen Damien that night in town said he appeared to be jovial, if a bit tipsy. But a few shared a very different opinion. As more witnesses came forward, some described him as being moody and angry. One or two even said they thought that Damien was under the influence of something stronger than alcohol. *Drugs.*

But how could they say for sure? They were all just opinions based on momentary conversations and interactions late on a Saturday evening. Some of these witnesses had been drinking themselves. Damien was being called merry and moody in practically the same moment, when we'd seen proof he was pleasant in Yorkies and he'd looked perfectly content eating his chips on the CCTV footage just after midnight. The accounts really didn't add up.

With all the information now in the hands of the police, there wasn't much we could do except keep Damien in the front of people's minds by speaking to local media and plastering posters around town. Initially his disappearance had sent shock waves round our little island home, but now things were starting to settle back into a sense of normality. We still had the support of our friends and neighbours, of course, but they had lives of their own to get back to.

Nothing changed for us, though. We were trapped in a bubble of fear and fragile hope.

With the CCTV evidence and a litany of witness accounts with the police for investigation, we prayed we'd have news soon.

Just over two weeks after Damien had gone missing, that prayer seemed to be answered, when three plain-clothed inspectors turned up at our home. One, named DC Clarke, was a big, broad man with the imposing stance of a *Star Wars* stormtrooper, while his female counterpart, DI Lesley Evans, was a short woman in her forties. We invited all three of them into our living room, so we could sit and talk more comfortably. DC Clarke and DI Evans followed, but the third officer lingered at the living-room door.

'Please,' I said. 'Take a seat.'

'I'm fine here, thank you,' he replied, leaning against the doorframe.

How unusual, I thought. It was like he was trying to blend into the background, not really participate. We sat around for a while, chatting about Damien and how things had been at home before he disappeared. I told them all about our shopping trip to Newport and how he'd recently started his new school. How we'd taken him to see his girlfriend Gemma in Suffolk during the recent half-term break, about two months after his little escapade with Jon. I'd seen pictures of Gemma and Damien was clearly smitten with her; he talked about her all the time.

Ed and I had found it so sweet and funny when we dropped him off. They were both bursting with excitement to see one another. Gemma was already waiting outside her house when we pulled up. Her parents must have been out at work, but we did get to meet her briefly. She was perfectly lovely and polite, but it was clear they wanted to be alone, so we made ourselves scarce.

As we continued to share the events of the weeks leading up to his disappearance, Sarah explained how, after visiting Gemma, Damien had popped in to visit her at university in Portsmouth.

'He stayed on the Thursday and asked if he could stay another night to go to a big party called the Renaissance Ball,' she explained. 'But I said no, because I couldn't afford to take him.' She'd called me and asked me to tell him to come home. 'I wish I'd let him stay now,' she sighed. I shook my head.

'This isn't your fault,' I said.

As the conversation continued, I mentioned the party at the house near Yafford Mill. I told the officers how those horrid kids had bullied Damien that night, but he'd asked me not to get involved. I explained how I couldn't see any possible connection at first.

'Maybe it affected him more than we thought,' I suggested. 'Someone from that party might know something?'

I told them how he'd started to really focus on his studies after getting great GCSE results and setting his sights on being a marine biologist. We talked about his friends and girlfriends. He certainly didn't seem to have any problems there. He'd split up with Abbie in the summer, just before meeting Gemma, but they'd remained firm friends.

In a way, it was nice to be talking about the overwhelming positives in Damien's life. To me it served to underline the fact that he had no reason to run away or want to vanish. That his disappearance was more than just 'a funny five minutes'. For once, it felt like some action was being taken. The officers explained that they had been assigned specifically to Damien's case. The investigation was to be called Operation Ridgewood. It was surreal, like something out of a movie. But it meant we were being listened to.

After a while, DI Evans, the female officer, explained what would happen next. She said that Damien's room and the rest of the house would need to be searched, and that some items might need to be taken for analysis. I nodded enthusiastically. Anything if it would help us to find Damien. Then she asked a question:

'Do you also mind if our colleague speaks to you all one at a time?' she said, gently. 'The children as well?'

'Not at all,' I said. But in that moment, I noticed something. DI Evans and 'Stormtrooper' had dominated the conversation, while this other officer had hovered in the doorway, barely uttering a word. I couldn't even recall his name, but I now nicknamed him DC Furtive. It seemed fitting. He'd been there the whole time, just watching us. Now he was going to interview us one by one? Realisation dawned on me – the investigation *had* finally begun. But they were starting the search with us.

Not with all the evidence we'd provided. Not with the clear leads. Damien's family. The same people who had been frantically searching while they'd been twiddling their thumbs.

I wasn't keen on this strange officer. He wasn't a run-of-the-mill policeman. It occurred to me that he probably had training in criminal psychology, reading body language and identifying strange tics and behaviours. As we'd spilled our guts to his colleagues, he'd been sussing us out, coming up with the questions he'd ask the kids in interview, no doubt. It left a bitter taste in my mouth, but we went along with it because we finally had their attention.

The officers took a brief look around Damien's room. DC Furtive interviewed Ed as they searched the attic. Storm- trooper took DNA swabs from all of our mouths and then the kids' interviews began. Sarah, being an adult herself, took the interview in her stride, while Melissa, at nine years old, simply did as we asked her.

'This policeman wants to ask you some questions about Damien,' I said to her. 'Will you be a good girl and speak to him in the kitchen? Mummy and Daddy will be just outside.'

'Yes, Mummy,' she'd said, keen to help in her own little way.

It was James who found the experience most difficult. Almost a teenager himself, in the months leading up to the night Damien disappeared, they'd grown closer. Rather than being the annoying little brother Damien would wrestle to the ground and tease mercilessly, they'd become friends. The loss hit him hard and he'd retreated into himself. He could barely talk to us about Damien, let alone a complete stranger from a police force that didn't seem to be doing much to help find his big brother. It was awkward for him, but still he did it.

They couldn't have made Ed and I prouder. But the experience as a whole disturbed us. Especially when it dawned on us that they were looking at us as suspects. In many ways, I under-stood why it had to happen and I was happy to work with them. We had nothing to hide, after all. We'd been nothing but open with the police. Virtually done their job for them. It was just the timing.

Why hadn't they done this two weeks ago, straight after I'd reported Damien missing? Why, until now, had we only seen the occasional uniformed officer when another pile of rags had been found? Why now, when we had new information that could easily shed more light on what happened? Why were they allocating manpower to scrutinising *us*, rather than trawling through the town centre CCTV footage? So much time had already been wasted.

The words of the lady from the Missing Persons Helpline haunted me: 'The first few hours are very important.' What hope did we have when the first few *weeks* had been handled so badly?

* * *

As time pressed on, each day without any news became harder than the last to deal with. The police assured us they were doing everything they could. As well as our family they interviewed friends and acquaintances, as well as witnesses they deemed to be credible. But how could we trust them? Our opinion of them was already tainted.

As the steady flow of daily visitors to our home began to dwindle, the silence and emptiness allowed the reality of Damien's absence in our lives to reveal itself. It was silly things, like not finding his sweaty socks strewn across the hall and not hearing him and James play-fighting upstairs. No guitar strumming or trombone blaring. Setting one less place for tea. Some days I sat and cried. Others I just sat for hours staring out of the window at the bus stop, willing Damien to step off every vehicle that stopped there.

Willing the nightmare to end.

But it never did.

I still believed the answer was out there. My bond to Damien, like all of my kids, ran deeper than I could explain. I'd always just *known* when something was wrong. In my gut I'd known since 8:30am on that Sunday morning that something was very wrong. But I was also sure he was still out there somewhere. I couldn't get the vision of him lying somewhere in the cold and mud, waiting for us to come and find him, out of my mind.

After a few weeks, Sarah decided to go back to Portsmouth, to keep up with her studies. Ed and I decided that James and Melissa needed to start getting back to something that resembled normality too, so we sent them back to school. They resisted at first, but after a few days they drifted back into routine.

It was a wrench for me. Since Damien had vanished, letting the kids out of my sight even for a few minutes terrified me. If they were even a second late I'd feel panic rising. They were good kids, though, and they did everything in their power to make sure I wasn't left worrying.

Melissa's school, Gurnard Primary, wrapped her in a cocoon of love and support. It broke my heart that a child so young and innocent had to experience her big brother simply 'disappearing', but she amazed us all with her resilience. On the hardest of days, her angelic little face was a ray of sunlight, breaking through the darkness. A few weeks after that, Ed sat me down.

'I think I should go back to work,' he said.

I felt sick at the thought. Too emotional to concentrate on anything, I'd had to give up the work placement I was doing as part of my college course. The people who had rallied around us at the start had returned to their normal lives. With the kids back at school and university and Ed working in London all week, I knew that my elderly parents would be round every day, but that didn't mean I wouldn't be alone with my thoughts and fears. But I knew it had to happen. His employer had been incredibly supportive, but there were limitations to the bounds of compassionate leave.

'I think you're right,' I agreed.

Our lives might have been frozen around that fateful morning in November, but the world went on around us. We still had bills to pay and food to put on the table. So, two weeks later, Ed returned to work. He called me three times a day, just to check in on me. But I couldn't bring myself to leave the house.

What if Damien rings while I'm out? a voice in my head said, whenever I considered the idea. So I sat by the phone, day after day, willing it to ring. I did what I could from home, continuing to speak to media and even being filmed for a documentary about missing people for BBC South. I'd never been the type of person who would be comfortable being on camera or speaking in public. In fact, I hated it. But I was willing to do anything if it might bring us closer to finding Damien.

Christmas was approaching too, which was something else to keep me busy. As a family we loved the festive season, but this year there was no happiness or excitement. How could we celebrate with the gaping hole that had been left in our world? That said I was determined to try. Even though Damien was missing I still had three other kids, all of whom deserved to feel even a little bit normal, despite everything we'd been through. And what if Damien *did* turn up one day? Imagine if he turned up on Christmas Day and there was no tree or decorations? No Christmas dinner or presents?

Somehow, we managed to go through the motions. We bought a beautiful real fir tree and decorated it with trinkets and baubles, including decorations that Damien and his siblings had made in school over the years. On the mantelpiece in the living room I hung six stockings embroidered with each of our names, including Damien's. Not hanging his stocking up would have somehow felt like an admission of defeat. Of giving up hope.

There was no chance that was happening.

Anyway, the idea of him not returning home was inconceivable. It would happen at some point, surely? As Christmas approached, I even managed to drag myself into town to buy the children some presents. I continued to try and keep Damien in people's minds, agreeing to speak to the *Isle of Wight County Press*.

'I just want him home for Christmas,' I told the reporter.

During our interview she asked me if I had a message for Damien, in case he read it.

I could feel a lump rising in my throat at the thought of being able to address him directly. To tell him how much we loved and missed him. I choked back tears as I spoke.

'It doesn't matter what's happened or what you have done, Damien,' I said. 'We just want to hear from you. Just please, please, come home.'

Later, a photographer came to take a picture to accompany the article. James, Melissa and I crammed awkwardly into a small corner of our living room, around our Christmas tree.

'Put your arm there . . . move closer . . . look sad . . .' As he snapped away, directing us into the perfect shot, I began questioning myself. It all felt absurd. I wanted to run out of the room, get this stranger out of my house. But instead I took a deep breath. I knew why I was doing it.

For Damien . . .

It was a way of reaching out to the community, to get them to recall that night. The story appeared in the paper on 13 December 1996.

'COME HOME FOR CHRISTMAS,' APPEALS FAMILY.

I wasn't sure what to expect. It was the first time I'd done a story that wasn't only an appeal for information. It was the first time we'd used the media to reach out to Damien directly. As the school term finished and companies shut for Christmas, the world around us slowed down.

The offices of Hampshire Constabulary were no exception. Officers took their annual leave and progress on the case ground to a halt. All we could do was wait.

CHAPTER SIX

C HRISTMAS DAY CAME AND WENT, BUT THERE WAS STILL NO CALL from Damien. The tinsel and trimmings were present in our little house, but joy had been absent. The empty chair at the table and unopened gifts under the tree had weighed heavily on us.

Damien was the joker of the family. He had a silly sense of humour that he'd inherited directly from his dad. Usually at Christmas he'd have us in stitches, lolloping about and telling jokes, teasing his siblings and pulling pranks on us all. Nothing could fill that gap. And we didn't want it to. We just wanted him back.

There was no fresh news from the police, either. The frustration and helplessness were overwhelming. Where holidays would usually fly by, the days dragged. All we could do was ruminate as the rest of the island celebrated. One night, Ed, Sarah and I were up talking about Damien. It was all we ever talked about any more, especially during those long, slow days during the festive break.

What else could we do?

I was churning over our family shopping day in Newport. But for once I wasn't trying to spot anything unusual about Damien's behaviour. I was questioning my own.

'Why did I go and get my hair done?' I lamented out loud. I could never have known, but that rare hour of 'me time' had stolen an extra hour I could have spent with Damien. When I got home, he'd been chatting away, but now I couldn't even remember what about. I'd been tired and distracted.

I wished I'd paid more attention.

And when he'd asked me if he could stay out until midnight, I wished I'd said no. God knows I'd wanted to.

'You wanted to let him grow up. We both did,' Ed said. 'We did exactly the right thing.'

I couldn't be convinced, though. The confusion, grief and regret left me numb. It was clear Sarah still felt the same about sending him home from Portsmouth a few days before that too.

'You can't blame yourself,' Ed said again, ever the voice of reason. 'This is no one's fault.' I guess he was right. We didn't even know what 'this' was. We had no idea what had happened to Damien, so how could we even start to assign blame?

Once again, our conversation turned to our questions about that night. About the things we'd been told in the weeks that followed his disappearance. The comments about Damien appearing to be on drugs still stood out to me as completely ridiculous, especially as the effects attributed appeared to be more closely aligned to something stronger.

'Damien wasn't interested in anything like that,' I said. 'I'm sure.'

Sarah shifted slightly in her seat and cast her eyes to the floor. Then she looked at me. 'I don't think he was on drugs, Mum,' she said. 'But . . .'

My stomach tightened slightly. *But what?*

Sarah took a deep breath and continued. 'We had a chat. He said he was interested in what it would feel like to take drugs.' I gasped, but Sarah continued before I could say anything.

'No, listen,' Sarah said. 'I talked it over with him and told him it was a terrible, dangerous idea. But I said that if he ever *was* going to do it, I wanted to be there to make sure he was okay.'

It turns out the chat had happened when Damien had last visited her in Portsmouth, just a few days before he disappeared. Looking at Sarah's stricken face, I knew she felt terrible betraying Damien's confidence.

'Did he ever try anything?' I asked. 'Apart from the pot?' Ed and I had once found a tiny amount of cannabis in Damien's room. When we confronted him about it he admitted to trying it. We were worried but not surprised when we found out. He was a typical, curious teenager. But after a stern talking-to about the dangers of drugs and the people involved, he'd apologised and promised it wouldn't happen again. But a bit of pot wasn't what Sarah was talking about here.

'I really don't think so,' she continued. 'We never spoke about it again.'

I knew how close they were. He knew he could trust Sarah and I had no doubt that if he'd wanted to act on his curiosity, Sarah would have known. I hugged her tightly.

'I'm glad you told us,' I said. I still firmly believed he was just drunk that night, but I knew that every tiny nugget of information was important. It was another step closer to building up the complete picture.

* * *

The year drew to a close and 1996 turned to 1997. There were no parties or fireworks for us, just a silent vow to continue doing whatever we could to find Damien.

January was cold and dark, the bleakness exacerbated by starting a new year without our eldest son physically present in our lives. Ed went back to work after the holidays, Sarah returned to uni and James and Melissa went back to school. I was alone again.

Damien never left my thoughts.

The police eventually shared two official theories with us. One was that Damien had simply run away of his own accord and perhaps didn't want to be found. The other was that he had drowned. Although there was no direct evidence to prove it, they seemed to think that he could have wandered towards the coast and simply fallen into the sea. Neither washed with me. There was an old saying on the island: *the sea gives back what it takes away.*

If Damien had fallen into the sea, surely his body would have washed up by now? Whenever a body or some human remains did appear on shore, the police came to us.

But it was never Damien.

Ed and my father had already been to speak to the harbour master, Henry Wrigley. They were aware that the Solent and its tides and currents were complex, but it was well charted too. The harbour master's opinion was in line with ours. If Damien had drowned, we would've known about it within days.

'They looked at the charts,' Ed had told me after their meeting. 'They calculated the tidal movements, the tidal sets and rate and a host of other factors, like the water temperature.'

I'd listened intently.

'He said the water had been cold that night, and that can sometimes mean it takes longer for a body to come to the surface. But not this long.'

Henry and his team had done everything that was physically possible, including providing us with a list of vessels that had been moored in Cowes Harbour on that night and when they left. I'd wondered if perhaps Damien might have been taken against his will. He would get seasick on vessels like those, so it's unlikely he'd have gone voluntarily. But it provided no answers and they found nothing. Damien never appeared.

Part of me was filled with joy. It was becoming increasingly unlikely that misadventure or an accident had led Damien to a watery end. But another part of my brain was screaming: *What did happen?*

Despite what the police seemed to think, I knew in my heart that he hadn't run away. Now an experienced seaman was telling me he was unlikely to have drowned. We were no further forward in our understanding than the day he'd not come home. I knew the police investigation was ongoing, but I couldn't leave it in their hands alone. Not after the mistakes that had already been made. With time on my hands, I set about looking at all of the information we had gathered.

We knew that Chris and Damien had left the party in East Cowes at around 9:15pm.

Curiously, one of the girls who'd been there had come forward to say she thought Damien had taken a camera from the house. She said he'd been taking photos of the party with it and hadn't wanted to let it go.

After the party the boys had gone to the Alldays shop. The girl working on the till that night had confirmed he'd bought three bottles of White Lightning. Turns out some of the kids he was with had given him money to buy the cider. They thought that because he was tall he'd stand a better chance of getting served.

Then they'd taken the *Jenny Lee* over to Cowes, a sighting that had been corroborated by two young girls who were on the boat at the same time. They'd described Damien as cheerful and chatty. After that, the information became complicated, with multiple sightings of Damien around town, much of it unverified. I did my best to create a timeline. I knew it might not be completely accurate, but it would show how Damien and Chris had made their way from the ferry along to the High Street.

At around 10pm, Damien was spotted in the Duke of York with other lads, then shortly afterwards in Yorkies, where he popped in and out without ordering. A few minutes later he was spotted smoking and drinking cider outside The Arcade with another boy, presumably Chris. A couple of friends said they saw Damien at around 10:20pm. One chatted to him outside The Fountain and said he was a little unsteady on his feet. Another saw him outside the Midland Bank and described him as 'merry' – not drunk.

In the space of about fifteen or twenty minutes, there were a number of accounts placing Damien in pubs around town, back at The Fountain, near the Three Crowns, in the Harbour Lights. One of the staff at the Harbour Lights recalled seeing him heading off along the seafront, in the general direction of Gurnard.

On his way home.

At half past ten, Damien had tried to get in The Fountain to see if Sarah was there. He'd been told to go away because he'd been eating chips. We still weren't sure where they had come from; we just knew that it wasn't Yorkies. But there was another chip shop in town. After that, accounts from the staff and CCTV footage placed him in Yorkies between 11:30pm and 11:40pm. This time he had ordered some chips – his second portion of the evening, if eyewitness statements were correct. The last recorded sighting of Damien came from the street CCTV at 12:02am. Walking along, eating his chips.

All this information was what was officially accepted, but there were reports of other sightings too. Sightings that didn't sit neatly in the timeline. Sightings that seemed to be attracting far less focus from the police, in my opinion.

He'd apparently shared chips with another witness at a bus stop by the Co-op on Denmark Road. At just before midnight a bus driver had claimed a lad in a dark jacket had got on the bus and asked to go to Cowes. He said the youth was unsteady on his feet and carrying a cheap camera and a portion of chips. When he informed him he was already in Cowes, the youth apparently thanked him and tried to take a picture with the camera but failed. He'd then apparently disembarked the bus with a smile. It sounded like the kind of daft thing Damien would do.

Another man, apparently a social worker, had been in his car waiting for his kids at that same bus stop. He claimed that a young man matching Damien's description had stumbled into his car and engaged him in conversation, saying, 'They're watching us.' The man said he hadn't a clue what he was talking about, before leaving when his kids didn't arrive.

But most compelling of all was a young man who claimed he'd seen a youth in the small hours, when he'd been making his way home from his parents' house. He'd been walking along Baring Road and had seen a person between Egypt Hill and the top of Woodvale Road, directly level with Solent Middle School. He said he resembled Damien's description.

Why wasn't more being done around this?

It wasn't easy getting hold of the police to share my concerns or ask questions. In fact, I hadn't seen DI Evans in quite some time. It was like she too had vanished off the face of the earth. It was a shame really. Most of the male officers we'd met were sharp and abrupt. She had a much warmer and gentler approach that I'd really appreciated. I had to wait until our stormtrooper, DC Clarke, came round again. When he did, I asked how the line of enquiry concerning the Baring Road sighting was progressing.

'*Pffft,*' he'd said, waving his hand. 'I wouldn't put too much on that.'

'Why not?' I asked.

'He's not a reliable witness,' he said. 'He's got previous.'

I was surprised. His response felt a little flippant. It was later than other sightings and no one else had reported seeing him in that area, but it was very close to where we lived. To me it felt relevant and plausible.

Surely worth looking into?

It began to niggle at me. It seemed that a new question would always arise just as we made progress in another area. *Missing,* the documentary I'd been filmed for around Christmas had finally aired, with an appeal for information about the men seen in Yorkies at the same time as Damien. The show had received an anonymous tip-off about two of them. It turned out they were in the army. When the police looked into it they said they couldn't be reached immediately, as one was in Australia taking part in a yacht race and the other away in Scotland on manoeuvres. I was certain it would be possible to contact them in some way, even if it wasn't a full interview. Just to ask them if they knew the other blokes in Yorkies. So I pushed on the police.

Maybe they could speak to the other men first, if they knew them?

I also reminded the police about the CCTV from the High Street cameras. Asked if these men could be seen on those. But nothing happened. I was so frustrated to see yet another hot lead being dithered over. To be let down again.

February came and went. After what felt like an eternity the police finally interviewed the two servicemen from Yorkies who had been identified by the tip-off. We'd waited with bated breath only to be told that the men didn't know anything, and they didn't know the other men in there at the time. They simply commented to Clarke that the others were not army men.

Another dead end.

My disillusion with the investigation so far had hit its peak. That was until an officer called DI Purvis gave an interview to the press about Damien. Initially I'd been delighted by the effort. Then I heard his comments. He said he believed Damien was probably alive and well and on the mainland somewhere. That he was probably just another teenager who had decided to run away from home.

I was seething. Was he *'probably'*?

It was an off-the-cuff comment, but to me the impact was seismic. Without any background or understanding about the case, someone could just dismiss Damien as a runaway. Not as a child who had mysteriously disappeared, completely out of character. Why were they so keen to push that version of events, even though it was far from proven? Media reports began purporting this theory as the most probable explanation. It was devastating, but it had come from the mouth of an officer of the law. How was I any match for that?

Despite nothing emerging from the two men who had been in Yorkies, there were still four more men to identify. What's more, the island rumour mill started to churn out more information about sightings of Damien. Some seemed plausible, while others were so outlandish and at odds with everything we knew so far, we simply didn't know what to make of them.

One rumour suggested Damien had been seen shouting up at the windows of a flat above the butcher's shop in town on the night he disappeared. The inhabitants were described as unsavoury types, but that was all hearsay. When I couldn't find the source of the story, I let it go. It didn't seem credible. We had far more serious things to worry about.

As well as sightings of Damien, we began to get tip-offs about what might have happened to him. One claimed some shady characters had beaten him up after he'd tried to defend a friend. It wouldn't have been the first time Damien had stood up for a friend. But which friend would this have been? Surely they would have come forward?

We also received an anonymous tip-off from a nurse at a local hospital. She called us to say she'd been looking after a patient who said he knew what had happened to Damien. The patient was a young man named Harry Corbett. He was addled by drug addiction, but the nurse said the things he was saying about Damien seemed coherent. She believed they were more than ramblings. Plus, she was risking her livelihood to tell us. Surely that counted for something?

'He said that he'd helped to bury Damien,' she said. 'And that his body had been wrapped in a carpet.' Naturally I was horrified by the suggestion. Not only did it suggest he'd been killed, it also suggested people had colluded to hide his body. I knew a drug addict wasn't the most reliable witness. But why would someone make something like that up?

It wasn't the only rumour of foul play. Another story suggested he'd come to harm at the hands of known paedophiles living on the island. Apparently some of them groomed boys by supplying them with drugs and booze. I shuddered at the thought. In my darkest moments, I had imagined that Damien may have been injured somewhere after an accident. Falling in the woods or over the cliffs. It had never crossed my mind that he might have been hurt by other people.

Until now.

The rumours gathered pace and became increasingly horrific. Before long there were multiple claims that he'd been killed and his body disposed of. We heard everything, from him being buried in the foundations of buildings on the island and being fed to pigs in the New Forest, to being chopped up and put into lobster pots off the coast.

Like something out of a horror movie.

The stories sickened me. But they were all unsubstantiated. They gave me the what, but not the why or how. As the stories took a darker twist, so too did my mind. I opened it to the unthinkable and began to ponder the seedier aspects of the island.

There were people I'd seen around town over the years that you just knew were involved in bad things. They looked like trouble. There was one girl in particular who sprung to mind. I didn't know her name, but she'd walk down the middle of Cowes' narrow High Street with her scary tattooed boyfriend and nasty-looking dog, straining on its leash. She was tall for a woman so she stood out. On more than one occasion I'd crossed the road to keep out of their way. They acted like they owned the place, but no one challenged them.

Now, hearing all these rumours about crime and drugs on the island, I wondered if they were players in that world. Could someone like that have hurt Damien? Had he possibly been in the wrong place at the wrong time? I couldn't see how it could be true. But I could no longer discount it either.

As the months passed I recorded every story that was shared with me, no matter how far removed it seemed from what we knew of Damien's activities that night. I passed it all on to the police. Everything was a possibility.

Damien's friends continued to rally round us. We wanted to keep him in the public eye, so we came up with creative ways to remind people of his story. National Missing Persons Helpline launched a campaign where missing people's pictures were put on the sides of milk bottles sold by Iceland, and Damien was included in this initiative. They even arranged for his face and an appeal to be put on the livery of Body Shop vans that drove all over the UK. I could only hope that it would bring more news.

We decided to organise a gig after Damien's close friend, Alex

Roberts, wrote a song about him. Alex and Damien had been friends since we'd moved back to the island in 1990. They both loved music and started their first band, Distorted Justice, as young teenagers. They'd spend hours jamming at Alex's house. Damien would sing and play the guitar and he loved every minute. The memory brought a smile to my lips.

My little rock star.

The song told the story of the good times they'd shared growing up and his hope for a happy ending, but for me it was the title that was most poignant – 'Someone Knows'. You see, I was sure that someone on the island DID know where Damien was. Looking at all the information, the rumours and speculation in front of me, I knew I had lots of pieces of a huge jigsaw. But I didn't have the picture to help me put it together. I didn't know how anything connected. That was what I had to find out.

Nine months after Damien vanished, we were still none the wiser as to what had happened to our son. Time marched on yet the investigation seemed to slow down. I took the decision to return to my studies. It wasn't that I'd given up hope; I just needed to do something else with my mind. I was so deep into the mire of rumour and speculation that I was being pulled under, barely able to cope. I had to stay afloat – for Sarah, James and Melissa. For Ed. And Damien, for when we finally brought him home.

Whatever that looked like.

Plus, Ed had bought me a mobile phone – a small blue brick with an extendable aerial. It was the first one anyone in our family had ever owned. It meant that I was contactable at any time if there was news about Damien from police or family. It gave me a new lease of life, but it tortured me too.

If Damien had had one of these . . .

It could have been so simple. When he found himself worse for wear, he could have just called us and asked us to pick him up. Or when he hadn't turned up at home the next day, we could have called him. The police might even have traced his phone to his location. This could've all been over, one way or another.

Eventually I completed my courses. Despite everything I'd been through, I'd managed to achieve NVQs in Office Administration and IT and was able to find a series of secretarial jobs to keep me occupied. I was so proud of myself, but working and maintaining a semblance of a 'normal life' was tough. People knew I was Damien Nettles's mother and it made some people uncomfortable. Employers and colleagues didn't always understand my frustration and anxiety. They weren't equipped to deal with what I was going through. I carried on, though, moving through jobs, keeping one eye on the investigation at all times.

Then, in January 1998, I received a phone call from DC Clarke. They had finally received new information. Information they could action. There was going to be a search, and it would be only a few hundred yards from our family home.

CHAPTER SEVEN

A S THE MONTHS HAD PASSED WE'D BEEN FORCED TO ACKNOWLEDGE the heartbreaking possibility that Damien might never come home. Not alive, at least. We knew there was a chance he'd had an accident. That we just hadn't found him yet. But we held out hope for better news and focused on the positives. The island gossip, however, continued to present more sinister possibilities.

Foul play. Manslaughter. Even murder.

I couldn't wrap my head around the idea. Nothing we knew for certain pointed to anything that could have involved Damien being killed by someone or something else, accidentally or otherwise. We'd already more or less disproved the idea that he'd fallen into the sea, although the police kept that line of enquiry open, notifying us whenever new remains washed up on the shore. The other major focus, for the police at least, seemed to be the idea that he'd run away.

But there were other leads being given far less focus, like the discovery that Damien's identity had been stolen in Torquay and used fraudulently to sign a Companies House notation. Local officers went to Torquay to verify this, but it was left with Torquay police to investigate, even when we learned that the alleged perpetrator was related to someone on the Isle of Wight. We were told the person would be interviewed, but then heard nothing more of it. We had to assume it was dealt with, but it felt like yet another hastily discounted line of enquiry.

Then there were the rumours – rumours we couldn't quash. Not without help.

Stories like how Damien was in the foundations of the new Grantham Court Flats on the seafront, or that he'd been buried down a cement mine in Stag Lane in Newport. The details that came with these stories were chilling. *He got dumped in the cement mine because he was too heavy to carry down the cycle track.*

But by whom? And why? I tried to understand where these stories might have come from. Did people just assume Damien was dead and get swept up in local gossip? Were they nasty, malicious stories designed to exacerbate our pain and distress? Or was there a germ of truth in them?

When Clarke told me about the plans for a massive police search of undergrowth in Gurnard, I forced myself to venture the question: 'Are you looking for a body?' I had no idea what new information they'd received, but it had certainly kicked them into action. Had they heard the same stories as I had? Found something within them that they could substantiate?

'We're considering all possibilities, Mrs Nettles,' he said.

'Yes, I know,' I said. 'What I mean is, are you considering it a murder case now?'

'This is still a missing person case,' Clarke replied. 'We have no reason to believe otherwise at this stage.'

My sigh of relief was only half-hearted. The police not considering the possibility of murder or even manslaughter should have been a good thing – a positive sign – but it wasn't. Not with the rumours I was hearing, all of which I'd passed over to them. Were they taking the information I was feeding them seriously? I'd seen how quickly they had dismissed information in the past, after all.

The search finally took place on the 15th and 16th of January 1998. Twenty-six police officers from the mainland and six tracker dogs swarmed through our peaceful little neighbourhood, going door to door to speak to residents. It took two days and was one of the biggest search efforts on the island for many years. Not that it brought much comfort.

They started with the sheds and outbuildings of every house, flat and chalet, including our own home, snaking out to the woods along the shore by the Solent School, tearing through the matted bushes. It was exactly the same place that Ed, James and my dad had gone the night after Damien first went missing. It had taken fourteen months for the police to sweep the same area. More than a year. What was it that had suddenly snapped them into action?

I still hadn't been able to get hold of DI Evans for an update. In fact, one officer suggested she'd left the force, but they couldn't tell me where she'd gone. It was frustrating. I knew that consistency was important to Damien's case. Changes to its assigned team would only cause problems and gaps in knowledge.

I asked DC Clarke about the search instead. He told me that new evidence had suggested that a youth resembling Damien's description was seen walking along Baring Road near to the Solent School, towards the top of our street, at about 12:30am on the Sunday morning. He'd apparently been seen carrying a plastic bag. I narrowed my eyes and frowned as I absorbed the information. Why did this sound so familiar? Then, suddenly, it hit me.

'This isn't new evidence,' I snapped. This was the exact same account that had been given by the witness that Clarke had dismissed in the first couple of weeks after Damien had vanished. It turns out that the man hadn't set back the clock in his car, so rather than 1:30am it was actually 12:30am when he thought he'd seen Damien. I was astounded. If they'd acted on this information immediately they would have known far sooner.

They could have done the searches earlier!

BBC South interviewed me about the activity. Not long after that I received a phone call from someone I'm calling, for the purposes of privacy, Simon W.

'Mrs Nettles,' the voice said. 'I want you to know I told the police I'd seen a lad that looked like Damien a few days after he disappeared.' I explained to him that I already knew about his account.

'I don't know why they didn't listen,' he said, frustration apparent in his voice. 'Things might have been different if they'd searched then.'

'I don't know either,' I said, not having the heart to tell him he'd been deemed unreliable.

Simon later spoke to BBC South and voiced his dismay at the fact his evidence had been discounted. Our local paper echoed my concerns, challenging the Chief Inspector in charge of the search, Phil Horn, about the slow response.

'I know there was criticism of us for not doing it before,' he told them. 'But searches were done, including that area, but not of this intensity.'

The only search I was aware of that took place in that area was by my family, I thought. Despite the extensive search though, nothing was found. No Damien. No body. No new leads. Might that have been different if the search had taken place in November 1996, rather than now?

We'd never know.

Once again the investigation seemed to grind to a halt. We were running out of ideas of how to turn up any new information. Our own door-to-door enquiries, community events, posters and flyers were delivering less and less. What came from them we already knew or was of little use. We'd tried everything. Well, almost everything. One day, at the start of March, Ed had a suggestion.

'What about a psychic?' he asked.

'A what?' I asked.

'A psychic,' he repeated. 'Someone who can try and get some otherworldly information.'

Ed had read about a renowned medium called Carol Everett, who'd played a part in a number of high-profile cases, found new clues and revived investigations.

'Surely it's worth a try?' Ed shrugged. I was worried. I wanted people to take Damien's disappearance seriously. Would this make us look wacky? Or just desperate? The truth was, we *were* desperate. We were running out of avenues to explore and the case was running cold.

We tracked Carol down to the mainland and Ed explained everything to her.

She was keen to get started but didn't want any further contact with Damien's family, in case it clouded her 'vision', so DC Clarke and his team acted as our go-betweens. We provided everything she requested: a photograph of Damien, a shirt and a sweater. I gave the officers a black and grey zip-up sweatshirt and a casual black pinstriped top that Damien loved to wear.

I had no idea what she did with them. I didn't really care. I just wanted to know what she could tell us. As we waited I remained sceptical, but I was willing to try anything. I wished for nothing more than to bring Damien home in time for his birthday on 21 June 1998.

He would be turning eighteen. A landmark birthday. He deserved to be home with his family.

Eventually, she came back to us with her findings.

'It seems he could be alive and well in France,' she said. 'The picture I have created seems to be related to a man who owns a boat.' My mind flitted back to the list of vessels that the Harbour Master had given us. Had we missed something there?

She'd drawn the place she believed Damien to be and a picture of another person that could be involved. The area in France she drew turned out to be a fairly accurate depiction of a quaint coastal town called Carnac in Brittany. But I didn't recognise the face of the other man. Considering the horror of the other theories we'd been presented with so far, I rather liked the idea of Damien living it up in a sunny French town. But it wasn't to be. The police took all the information and shared it with Interpol, in case anything could be verified, but nothing came back.

After that, the investigation limped along. I filled my time doing interviews that I believed could make a difference – for the *Mail on Sunday* supplement *You*, as well as *Best* and *Woman's Own*, which had been organised by National Missing Persons Helpline. It was draining and emotional, but I did it anyway. I wasn't about to let my boy be forgotten. If I could keep him in the public eye, there would be more chance someone might remember *something*.

We didn't hear much else from the police again until April, when a body washed up at Calshot Beach, near Southampton. It was almost routine now. A body would appear and the police would prepare us to expect the worst. At first it had filled me with grief and anguish, fear and desperation. Now it was just our 'normal'. A strange state of having one foot back in 1996, forever waiting for the most unthinkable news, and another in the present, plodding along on the school run and to the supermarket, typing and filing and work, all those little day-to-day mundanities.

Another man from the island, a 64-year-old called Edwin Wilcox, had also gone missing. The consensus was that this body would be either Damien or him. Eventually, the call came.

'It's not Damien,' the officer told me. The cursory wave of relief washed over me, tinged with the grief of still not knowing where our son was. Then it was back to normal. Or 'our normal', at least. We later found out that it wasn't Edwin Wilcox either. As the news sunk in we were left with more questions and yet another endless wait.

As time had moved on, I'd learned there were hundreds of us. The National Missing Persons Helpline had helped me to speak to countless journalists about Damien for newspapers and magazines, to radio and TV. As I'd done so I'd met more and more families of other missing people. Children and adults.

One day, as I waited in the green room before appearing on *Kilroy*, the enormity of the missing people community suddenly dawned on me. There were maybe a dozen families, including the father of a girl called Dinah McNicol. She'd been missing since 1991 and had appeared on the same poster as Damien, just above Richey Edwards. We were all out there, going for months without news, hopes being shattered as leads went cold, isolated in our anguish. After the initial rush of support the rest of the world would move on while we remained suspended in limbo. A state of *ambiguous loss*.

It was a term I had only come across since Damien had gone missing, coined by a researcher called Dr Pauline Boss in the 1970s. It meant a loss that left you without understanding of how or why it had occurred. A loss that left you searching for answers and unable to grieve. That's where we were. And what it felt like to be the family of a missing person.

'We are all members of a club that no one wants to join,' Dinah's father had piped up as we chatted. He'd hit the nail right on the head.

* * *

Before we knew it, Damien's eighteenth birthday arrived – a momentous life event that should have been filled with fun and laughter, with pride at our little boy growing into a man. Instead it was just another day without our handsome, silly boy.

It was Father's Day too. I couldn't even imagine how that must have made Ed feel.

'Are you okay?' I asked him gently. Ed shrugged as the sombre mood pervaded our house.

'It'll never be the same without Damien here,' he said, sadly.

I hugged him tightly, willing to ease some of his pain, but I knew I couldn't. It was a day that should have brought him nothing but joy for his children. Twenty months had passed and I think that Ed and I had cried inwardly for him every day. But there were times when we just couldn't hide the tears from the kids. We were too overwhelmed by the loss.

On the night of his birthday, Ed, Melissa, James and I gathered at home. We tried to imagine what Damien would want us to do. I bought a card and made a cake, but none of us felt much like eating it. As with any landmark date, the *County Press* were keen to speak to us. They wanted to mark Damien's birthday and talk about the findings of the psychic from earlier in the year. I appreciated the support, but this time I felt flat. I didn't feel like it was going to lead anywhere. Nothing had so far.

So what was the point of parading our grief like this?

I couldn't risk not doing it either.

'I keep on hoping that eventually the publicity will jog someone's memory,' I told the reporter eventually. 'I honestly, truly, think someone, somewhere knows something about Damien.'

Then, I think for the first time ever, I admitted something I'd tried hard not to accept. Not because I didn't want it to be true, but because I didn't see *how* it could be true.

'Either he has met a sticky end and been the victim of foul play at someone's hands,' I said, 'or someone has helped him to leave the island.'

I prayed it would be the latter. But I had to find out either way.

CHAPTER EIGHT

Towards the end of the year, in October 1998, we did get the answer at least to one mystery – the case of the missing DI Evans. Lesley had mysteriously vanished a few months after she'd been assigned to Damien's case and no one from the police had really been able to tell me where she'd gone. I'd wanted to know in case there was anything we might need to check with her. But with everything that had gone on, chasing that up had fallen low on my list of priorities. Then, one day, I popped into the shop and spotted a news story splashed across the front page of the *County Press*: SEX TAUNTS MADE ME QUIT CID, CLAIMS WPC.

Intrigued, I picked up a copy and scanned the story. My jaw almost hit the floor. A detective from Hampshire Police had successfully taken the force to an industrial tribunal after suffering sexual harassment at the hands of colleagues. It was described as 'workplace bullying of the worst kind'. The victim had been handed one of the largest compensation awards for sexual harassment at the time. What's more, the abuse had taken place while the detective was working on a 'high-profile missing person case'.

It had to be Damien's. It had to be DI Evans!

I didn't know of many female detectives on the island. Come to think of it, I'd only ever met her. Eventually I found another article, this time in the *Independent*. It confirmed my suspicions: 'Hampshire Police paid a six-figure sum to Lesley Evans, 37, who was the only woman officer working with 22 men in the CID department in Ryde, on the Isle of Wight,' the story read.

The details turned my stomach. On one occasion, one of her colleagues had leaned against her and simulated sex 'like a rutting pig'. The same officer had also dropped his trousers in front of her. When she'd complained, her superior had laughed it off. Treated it like banter.

Despite having not always felt like the police had done the right thing by us, I was devastated to hear how she'd been treated. As a woman, I felt the burn of her humiliation and shame and anger towards those men. No woman should ever endure that behaviour anywhere, let alone in her workplace. But as the mother of a child whose case was in her care at the time of the abuse, I felt a wave of other emotions.

How could she have concentrated on her job with all this happening?

Might things have been overlooked?

Could the stress have caused her to miss things?

Then I was filled with pure outrage and disgust. I'd entrusted this force to try and find my son. At the time we were begging for them to help us, this was going on. They weren't even capable of basic human standards, let alone professional ones. What a shambles!

So many mistakes had been made in Damien's case right from the start. They'd dismissed me as a hysterical mother from the off. They clearly had no respect for women. I knew that not every officer in the force had been involved. There were some 'good ones', even if they'd not yet proven particularly effective. Officers like DC Clarke, for instance. But the fact that this had been allowed to happen brought the whole constabulary under scrutiny. I couldn't help but wonder: had they always upheld professional standards in Damien's case? Done the right thing, at the time it should have been done? It didn't feel that way.

A few weeks later, my private concerns appeared to be justified. An officer called DCI Ray Burt popped round to our house to say he'd be reviewing Damien's case. He was a new face to me but he'd apparently been working the case behind the scenes. Nothing was mentioned about Evans's departure. As we chatted, I asked about the CCTV from the town centre cameras.

Since the day we'd watched the footage at the Marina, I had been convinced that the tapes from earlier and later in the evening would provide us with more context, if not answers.

'It was sent to Netley Police HQ for enhancement,' DCI Burt said. 'I'll chase it up.'

Netley was the local HQ where forensics and the like were sent. The CCTV footage seemed to have been there a lifetime. I waited patiently until I received news from Burt.

'Mrs Nettles,' he said. 'Unfortunately the CCTV footage from the Marina has been lost.'

'Excuse me?' I gasped.

'It has been lost,' he repeated. 'The tapes were left in the Marina and eventually taped over.'

So they had never been sent to Netley? There was a tape or two in particular that contained the sighting of Damien. But I'd assumed that Sergeant Goodall had 'bagged and tagged' all of the tapes that night at the Marina. *Wasn't that what happened with evidence?* Instead, he'd left them there that night with a sticky note reading 'keep for police'.

The officers explained that the tapes could only be viewed on the Marina video machines, so they had been left to one side, but somehow they had found their way back into circulation, as the town council had needed them to keep the cameras running. The police claimed they had been reused.

I was shocked into silence. Bewildered beyond belief. *They'd left a 'sticky note'?* This wasn't a reminder to send a fax or pick up some milk. It was evidence in a missing person case!

After the initial shock wore off, I was incensed. Angrily, I wrote an email to DC Clarke and DCI Burt saying that I wanted to make a formal complaint. It was just one mistake too many. A few weeks later, Clarke and another officer turned up at St Mary's Hospital, where I was working, with a written statement from Sergeant Goodall.

'We wanted you to see this,' Clarke explained as we sat in the cafeteria. I read the statement carefully. He said that he was 'very sorry' if the loss of the tapes had caused any 'upset', but sent his assurances that the tapes had contained 'nothing of any operational value'.

My heart broke for Damien. I tried to remain calm but this man had lost vital evidence pertaining to my son's case. How did he know there was 'nothing of any operational value' in them? Since those tapes had last been viewed we'd unearthed far more information. Information that those tapes could have corroborated or disproved. They could have put an end to the hell my family was enduring. The impact this might have had on Damien's investigation was too great. He needed to be held accountable, so I submitted my complaint.

Time pressed on. In the end there was a local resolution to my complaint. Sergeant Goodall had 'received guidance' on how the loss of the CCTV might have impacted Damien's case. He was to be retrained in handling evidence of that kind, so the same mistake wouldn't be made again. It was barely a slap on the wrist. And it did nothing to help us at all.

It seemed all we had was either bad news or no news. That was until April 1999, when something positive happened. We found out we were going to get the one thing we'd been desperate for in the weeks after Damien had vanished. A reconstruction.

After all our campaigning a local ITV reporter called Dave Russell got in touch with us and offered to film a reconstruction of Damien's last steps. He'd reported on Damien's case since the start, so was familiar with all of the twists and turns. We were so grateful he'd been able to secure a slot for it to be broadcast, even if it was only at the end of the afternoon news, when most people would be in work or school. It was something and it meant a lot to me.

Everything was arranged. All they needed was someone to play Damien.

'I know just the person,' I said to Dave. I picked up the phone and called my friend Elaine Butler. 'Can I ask a huge favour of Duncan?' I began.

Elaine lived in Gurnard too. She had three children each around the same ages as Sarah, Melissa and Damien. They all knew one another and had played together growing up. It wasn't only that they were friends – Duncan was eighteen and the spitting image of Damien. Even before he'd gone missing, if I saw him around town I'd do a double take, thinking the tall, gangly figure was Damien. He would be perfect. Elaine and Duncan agreed. They were more than happy to help.

When the time came for the reconstruction to be filmed, I went into town to watch.

Clarke was there too, assisting Dave, and also taking care of a rather unpleasant chap who took it upon himself to stand on the sidelines and hurl obscenities.

Seeing it all come together felt like a light at the end of a very dark tunnel. After it was broadcast we were on the edge of our seats, waiting for news to come in. In the end, though, it managed to muster only a couple of calls, both from people who thought they might have seen Damien after the time of his disappearance. Neither checked out. It was another enormous disappointment.

We'd rolled with the punches from the start of the inquiry. Every time we were knocked down, we got back up and carried on. Every time we hit a wall, we turned around and found another route. But almost three years on it was getting harder to do. Especially when we had more bad news.

The firm that Ed worked for had been hit hard by changes in the economy. They'd been forced to lay off some staff. Ed had been one of them. There were far worse things that could happen than losing a job – we knew that only too well. New jobs could be found a great deal more easily than missing sons. However, it didn't change the fact that we still had three other children to feed and put through school, and a roof to keep over our heads. That couldn't be done on my modest secretary's salary alone. Not for long, anyway.

VALERIE NETTLES

Ed set about furiously applying for jobs, then waiting
anxiously for news. It was an added strain on the creaking
foundations of our family. I was struggling to cope and I
hadn't slept properly since the night Damien had vanished.
The strange, unconnected pieces of information surrounding
his disappearance swirled constantly in my head. My mind was
never at rest. I was always questioning: *Why? How? Who?*

Even at times when I was relaxing, a seemingly inconsequential
piece of information imparted by a friend or stranger would
trigger something in my mind. Not alarm bells, exactly. More a
gut sense that it was a part of the puzzle. That it would at some
point be relevant. It happened one day when I was swimming
with Chris's mum, Conny Boon. We'd stayed in touch over the
years, and would sometimes go to Gurnard Pines for a swim in
the morning before I headed to work. We'd been chatting, about
everything and nothing really. Then one day she mentioned
something that made my ears prick up.

'There's this house at the other end of our street,' she said.
'There's always young kids going back and forth. It's very odd.'

The Boons lived on Fellows Road. It was a long street made
up of older homes that had been made into flats or bedsits,
alongside newer flats and private residences that were rented
or owned. It made for a real mix of characters up and down the
street, from families like the Boons to more transient residents
who seemed to lay roots nowhere.

She'd explained how the man who lived there was a big
man, in his thirties, and by all accounts a nasty piece of work.
It was information like this that made me realise there was an
underworld thriving on the island. An underworld that might
have had something to do with Damien's disappearance. Not

95

that we'd had much news to confirm or deny such a rumour.

When I checked in with police regarding leads that we'd passed over to them, they insisted that all viable information had been followed up, but to no avail. They even claimed that their paid criminal informants hadn't turned anything up. Something they told me was a rarity. I was sceptical. Had they really passed on everything we'd told them, or cherry-picked the information they deemed 'reliable'? Or were they just worn-out cops getting by, waiting for their pensions?

My doubts meant I couldn't leave it in their hands alone. They'd let us down too many times. We needed to keep searching and investigating too. The debacle over the town centre CCTV a few years earlier started to play on my mind again. I began to ask around. I wanted to verify some of the things I'd been told by the police about how the CCTV was managed. In time I was directed to a man called Rod Ainge. He was in charge of CCTV for the council. I tracked him down to a local cafe and told him what the police had said.

'They told me that the tapes must have found their way back into circulation,' I explained. 'They said the town council had needed them to keep the cameras running. They claimed they had been reused.'

'That's not right,' he said. 'We have two spares, so we can carry on operating the cameras even if a couple of tapes need to be taken away. Also, I remember the logbook showed that the police had signed those tapes out, but never back in.'

Unfortunately the logbooks were discarded every couple of years. The ones from 1996 were long gone. But the information Rod had shared made me suspicious. Were the police trying to palm off the blame on to the council?

There were also still gaps in Damien's movements on that night. Constant rumours that something more sinister had occurred after he'd last been spotted. But there was no evidence. Nothing more to go on. The hopelessness left me unable to sleep or eat. I was struggling to concentrate at work and eventually I found myself at my doctor's. Everything that I was feeling poured out.

How guilty I felt about bringing Damien back to the island.

How I regretted extending his curfew.

How I felt let down and belittled by the police.

How I felt like we had nowhere left to turn.

'Mrs Nettles,' the doctor said, 'you need to speak to someone about these feelings. A professional.' He referred me to an NHS counsellor.

'She's a mother,' he said. 'She'll understand your feelings.' Reluctantly I went along. Every week for ten weeks. The counsellor was a consummate professional, as well as caring and nurturing, but it didn't change the way I was feeling. I didn't need sympathy. I needed help.

Another ten-week session was offered with a different counsellor. Another woman. But she wasn't gentle or soft. In fact, she was harsh, but she made me question my emotions. Sort fact from fiction. Useful from the useless.

'I just feel that if I hadn't moved us back here this never would have happened,' I said one day. 'The guilt is too much.' The counsellor stopped me abruptly.

'Why do you feel so much guilt?' she asked.

I examined the thought again. Our counselling sessions had mainly been about Damien but, as we talked, other aspects of my life, current and past, came out. She encouraged me to confront my thoughts and feelings – to own and be empowered by them. My mind turned first to Sarah, who I knew felt the same guilt about not letting Damien stay with her just before he vanished. Then I remembered something else, from way back in my own childhood.

It was the summer of 1969, when Neil Armstrong was on his way to the moon. We were living in America and my nana had flown from England to see us. It was the first time she'd ever taken a plane. But while she was visiting there was a terrible accident.

She'd got up early to make a cup of tea and her clothes caught fire, leaving her with second- and third-degree burns over forty per cent of her upper body and face. That day, my little sister, Sally-Anne, who was four years old, and I sat on the stairs of the apartments in shock, while our parents went to the hospital with Nana. Dazed and alone, our neighbours took us in.

Nana was in Charity Hospital in New Orleans for weeks with my mother and father at her bedside. My little sister Sally and I stayed with friends, away from the fire-damaged kitchen and acrid smell of burning flesh that had filled the apartment. As if things couldn't get worse, Hurricane Camille struck. We had to evacuate the city and leave Nana in the hospital. The decision broke my mother's heart, but we had little choice. Our whole family was at risk. So we fled.

Two days later we returned to our storm-ravaged town. Nana, thankfully, was okay. She had pneumonia but was still hanging on. But our joy didn't last long. Later that month she passed away after succumbing to complications with the pneumonia.

'My mother brooded over the fact that the accident would not have happened had we not moved to America,' I said to the counsellor, as I reached the end of the tale.

'What do you think about that?' the counsellor asked.

'That it wasn't her fault,' I said. 'That if it wasn't that it could have been something else, somewhere else.'

The counsellor nodded and I understood. I needed to release myself from the guilt. It wasn't helpful. It was holding me back.

Damien's disappearance wasn't my fault.

In time her sessions helped. I began to realise that my emotions were, and had always been, valid. That I didn't need to question that panic I had felt from the very moment I'd gone to the police. That I wasn't a 'hysterical mother'. I was a woman suffering a terrible loss. I had a right to experience and show emotion – as much now as back at the start. I felt empowered. And ready to keep fighting. Finally, as well, Ed had some good news.

'I've been offered two jobs,' he announced.

'That's wonderful,' I said. He'd had plenty of interviews but had suffered so many rejections at the last hurdle. At last he had the success he deserved. And with a choice!

I was filled with pride.

'There's just one thing,' he said, shuffling on the spot.

'Go on,' I replied.

'They're both in America,' he replied. 'One in Chicago, one in Dallas.'

They're what?

I'd known Ed had cast the net wide in his search. But moving back to America? I'd never entertained it. Even if Damien were still with us I'd have challenged it. We'd come back to the UK to lay some roots, give the children some stability. But the fact that Damien was missing? That compounded my resistance to moving away even further.

'How can we leave?' I said. 'Damien is still here somewhere.'

'We have to live,' Ed reasoned. He was a practical person, as well as emotional.

But I dug my heels in. There was no way I was leaving the island without knowing what had happened to Damien. Ed persisted and we discussed it as a family. James felt the same as me. Plus, he'd just turned sixteen and didn't want to leave his friends and start again. Melissa and Sarah, on the other hand, were thrilled by the idea. For Melissa, it was a huge adventure. For Sarah, it was an escape. She'd recently come out of a long-term relationship and was more than ready for a change.

We revisited the idea over and over. Ever so slowly, I began to crack. Seeing the excitement on the girls' faces, a glimmer of joy that hadn't been present in so long, made me think: it wasn't only about me. Developments in technology meant there were now ways I could keep in touch with the police and media about the investigation. The job had a good salary, and flights to and from the USA were pretty reasonable so, if I needed to come home, I could be back within a day. Plus, we had family on the island too.

In the end, Ed accepted the job in Dallas. He was to be the managing director of a large international freight forwarder. He planned to move out first, in November. All being well, he suggested that we follow in July 2001, when Melissa and James's school year had ended. It was a wrench, but maybe it was the best thing for all of us.

Reluctantly I agreed. If I refused and we stayed, we'd have lost the house anyway. Plus, the kids needed to be with their dad.

It was decided: we were moving back to America.

CHAPTER NINE

JUST BEFORE ED MOVED TO START HIS NEW JOB, OUR LATEST SENIOR Investigating Officer – or SIO – DI Dave Stewart, came to our house to provide an update on Damien's case. He had recently been promoted and was preparing to hand the case over to a new SIO.

We were told that the case had been reviewed and a number of recommendations had been made. These included looking at DNA evidence using new techniques that hadn't been available when Damien first went missing, researching naval ships that had been in port on that night, to try and identify the other men in Yorkies, and searching some of the potential 'grave' sites that had come from talk around the island.

It gave us some hope. Even though we were moving away, they seemed to be continuing the investigation rather than sweeping it under the carpet. I just hoped that this new SIO, DCI Williams, would maintain the pace.

Weeks turned to months and it was soon time for Ed to

leave. After Ed left, it wasn't easy. The financial burden improved, but not really enough to maintain two homes, and we all missed him terribly. Even though he was always on the phone, it wasn't the same. He missed us too, but we muddled along. Ahead of our move, I kept myself busy. I set up an MSN email address, so I'd be easily contactable after my move. I made sure everyone had it – the police, local journalists, even people who had already come forward with information. I wanted them to know that I wasn't giving up on my search. Out of sight, maybe, but not out of mind. Between that, my full-time job and bringing up the kids, the time flew by.

At first, Ed rented an apartment with another guy who had also moved to work with the company. In the Easter of 2001, Melissa, Sarah, James and I went over to visit. It was clear that the girls felt at home immediately. But James was not so keen.

'I don't want to move here, Mum,' he said to me. His position hadn't changed since the first day the idea had been floated. When we returned to the Isle of Wight, the conversation continued. James wanted to stay on the island. I completely understood why.

I'd been uprooted from the island and all of my friends myself at the age of fifteen. It had been upsetting, stressful and scary. I'd missed my friends. I hadn't resented my parents for it, but it had been difficult. Not a happy time for me at all. This was supposed to be James's first summer of freedom. He was about to finish his GCSEs. He had a close circle of friends. There were places he liked to go and people he liked to see. He didn't want to walk away from all that. He was in exactly the same stage of life as Damien had been when he'd gone missing. Finding himself, his place in the world. Testing boundaries. He had his life set up and he didn't want any of that to change.

The dilemma tore me apart inside. Did I allow him the freedom to grow up, or force him to come with us? If Damien hadn't disappeared, would we even have questioned James staying? Probably not. But I'd had to make this choice once before – on a far smaller scale.

'Can I stay out until midnight?'

The memory sent a shiver down my spine. I'd agreed to that, and then I'd never seen my son again. How could I make this decision? The thought of leaving James alone with his grandparents on the island – knowing how Damien had just vanished – was too much. What if I agreed and something terrible happened to James too? It didn't bear thinking about.

Ed and I agonised over the decision for weeks on end. But eventually, we came to a decision. James had been through enough. Losing his brother, living in a goldfish bowl, dealing with the constant speculation about what might have happened to Damien. Despite all that, he'd managed to carry on with his life, make friends and feel something that had at least a semblance of normality.

How could we deprive him of that?

In the end, we agreed he could stay on the Isle of Wight with his grandparents, on the condition that he listened to them and called us regularly. After that, time seemed to speed up. Just before we packed up the house, the children decided they wanted to do something to acknowledge they were leaving the home they had shared with their beloved brother.

And in the year that he should have turned twenty-one.

'Let's throw a party,' said Sarah. 'Damien would have loved that.'

'Yeaaaaah!' said Melissa.

I loved the idea. It seemed a fitting way to say goodbye, so we set to planning. It was very impromptu – just a barbecue in the garden with food and drink. We invited our friends and family, as well as people who had supported us in the search for Damien, like Auriele and Sophie from the National Missing Persons Helpline. It was simple, but special. Our home was full of people old and young, all united by their love for our family. *For Damien.*

We laughed, we sang, we cried. Most importantly, we got to say our goodbyes.

When local journalists got wind of our plans to return to America, they once again asked me for an interview. I agreed, of course, but it felt even tougher than usual. Maybe it was because I was still wrestling with my decision to go. The truth is, I felt absolutely abysmal.

I explained our decision as best I could to the reporter. I said it was a mixture of financial necessity and hope for creating a better future for Sarah, Melissa and James. During the interview, they asked me if I thought Damien was still alive. I paused for a moment. It was an anguished question that had rattled through my brain day and night for the past four and a half years. Logic told me it was unlikely. But my heart was a whole other story. I tried to give a measured response.

'Having no evidence otherwise, you just have to hope that by some quirk of circumstance he is out there somewhere,' I said eventually.

When the story was published, I spotted that DI Stewart had also been quoted. He'd told the paper that the inquiry into Damien's disappearance was ongoing and that police efforts were even being redoubled. We had been made aware of the fact that they were looking at using new techniques, such as DNA testing, which hadn't been available when Damien first disappeared. The talk was all well and good, but we hadn't seen much action.

As well as pointing to the potential for DNA, DI Stewart also appealed to Damien's friends, acquaintances and those who had been teenagers themselves at the time for new information.

'In 1996 Damien's peers were sixteen and seventeen,' he said. 'Now they are that much older – some may even have children of their own now – they may feel able to tell us something they were not prepared to divulge as teenagers.'

He was right. I'd always felt that not everyone had shared *everything* that happened that night – even some of Damien's closest friends. I wondered if there was something or someone they were scared of. Something that maybe now didn't pose as much of a threat?

Maybe now they would be able to come forward.

* * *

Before we knew it, it was time to box up our belongings for the big move. I was overwhelmed by the thought of unpacking in a place that I didn't know. A place I didn't want to be going to. But I pressed on. I had to.

With the help of James and Melissa we tackled Damien's bedroom. Over the years the room had been shared by the girls, then the boys, until they grew a little older. That's when we had turned the extension into a bedroom for James. The other room became Damien's private space. There were things that belonged to the whole family still squirrelled away in the overstuffed, built-in cupboard. But it was Damien's room. We'd left it just as he had the last time he left the house. It wasn't a shrine exactly; just a small part of the world that still felt like him. We began to prepare his things for the journey. Every single item that belonged to him was gently scrutinised, held close and hugged tightly.

It was all we had left of him.

School papers were sifted through once again, as we searched for the slightest hint about what might have happened to him. A clue. We read his personal letters to girlfriends, notebooks filled with song lyrics, even his fishing magazines, just one more time, in case he'd doodled anything down. But we found nothing. Final search over, we packed everything. Nothing was left behind.

Except, of course, for Damien himself.

The removal van arrived and men shuttled to and from the house with furniture, crockery, appliances and box after box of our belongings. We helped, picking up smaller bits and making plenty of cups of tea. Eventually there was only one more box to collect. I climbed the stairs one last time, running my fingers over the banisters. Damien's fingerprints were all over this house. Leaving it felt wrong, like I was leaving the last parts of him. My heart was heavy as I walked into my bedroom. I scooped up the last brown box and turned on my heel.

Suddenly, there was a noise: *THUD!* It echoed around the walls of the house, now completely empty of any evidence of our family's life there. Something had fallen out of the box. I glanced over my shoulder. There was a small blue booklet on the floor. Looking more closely, I realised what it was. A passport. *Damien's American passport.*

I put the box down and reached to grab it. It had fallen open on the page with his picture. I honestly felt my heart tear in two, as I looked at the photograph. He was only about six at the time it had been taken. Every inch of me ached to hold him as I picked up the passport and traced his face with my finger. His big eyes were staring at me. It was like he was calling out to me.

'Mum, don't leave me.'

The sense of unfinished business overwhelmed me. The devastating feeling that I was abandoning my first born son; a piece of my own heart. I hurt to the core. The anguish and emotion was indescribable. But I sucked in a deep breath. The decision had been made and there was no going back. I would deal with this. Like I had dealt with everything the last four years had thrown at me.

I would deal with it for Damien.

Just because I was leaving the island it didn't mean I was abandoning him. How could I leave something – some*one* – that was a part of me? My own flesh and blood? As long as there was breath left in my body I would search for him. I would leave no stone unturned.

I *would* find out what happened to him.

* * *

The girls slipped easily into life in America. We bought a house in the town of Flower Mound in Texas and Melissa started Flower Mound High School in early August, at the beginning of the fall semester. She found it strange initially but she soon made some good friends. She loved the American high school life. It was what she'd longed for after years of watching television shows like *Saved by the Bell*.

Sarah found a good job with the computer company

Compuserve almost immediately after we arrived. She found a circle of young British expats who had also moved across the pond with their families, as well as American friends, male and female, who were fascinated by her British accent and pretty appearance. They all thought she was 'cute'.

For me the transition wasn't so easy. Once we were unpacked and the house was in order, my mind turned back to Damien's case. Without me prodding the police along, was anything being done at all? I made sure they didn't forget me. I emailed regularly for updates and called when I could. I made it clear that I could fly home at the drop of a hat, if need be. Flights were cheap enough, and with Ed back at work the financial implications didn't overly concern me.

After a month, James decided he wanted to come out and join us. He'd had his fun over the summer, but he missed us. Said he needed to be with his family. *Or at least he thought he did.* He seemed to have difficulty settling anywhere, to be honest. But that was understandable, considering what we'd been through as a family.

We were over the moon. Life wasn't quite the same without him. Having him back would fill one of the gaps in our little family. We knew his mind was by no means made up, but we were glad he was trying. It gave me one less thing to worry about.

James flew out in August and his cousin Sophie and my brother Nigel also came out to see us, flying in on 10 September 2001. The next day, terrorists flew two planes into the twin towers of the World Trade Center. The attack killed 2,977 innocent victims. Overnight the world became a much more frightening place. We were glued to our TV screens as events unfolded, horrified that such obvious evil existed.

We lived under the flight path of Dallas/Fort Worth International Airport. Usually planes would jet over us at regular intervals, but after 9/11 there was silence for days. We felt so lucky that Nigel and Sophie had flown a day earlier. Although their flight number was completely different, we also knew how easily it could have been them.

The aftermath of 9/11 meant that airfares shot up in price. Looking at the cost of catching a flight home began to make me nervous. If Damien were to turn up would we be able to afford to get home immediately? We'd have to find a way.

Not long after moving we had some positive news from the police back on the Isle of Wight. The investigation had a new SIO, DCI David Williams, and it had been transferred from the Isle of Wight police force to Hampshire Constabulary's Major Crimes Unit in Fratton, on the mainland.

We were pleased, but when we first heard, only one question came to mind – what 'major crime' were they investigating? Despite numerous people making the suggestion of foul play over the years, Damien's case had remained a missing person case. Had something now changed? I asked our new SIO, David Williams, directly.

'Does this mean Damien's case is a murder case now?' I asked. The thought alone raised my hopes for a more targeted investigation.

'Oh no,' he replied. 'It's still a missing person case. It will remain that way until we have firm evidence of foul play. We're still considering all scenarios.'

It was frustrating, but at least it was in the hands of the team that looked after that sort of case. As part of the transferral to Major Crimes, I also learned that details of Damien's case would be entered into the HOLMES database. I investigated what this meant. Although I'd heard the name before, I didn't really know what it was. Before all this, why would I have needed to?

Eventually I stumbled across a detailed description of HOLMES. I could have punched the air with joy. In a nutshell, it was a system designed to improve the effectiveness and productivity in crime investigations. Something I felt Damien's case seriously needed. Maybe once the information gathered over the years was added to HOLMES it would highlight some new information, provide some new leads to follow? It might show links and connections to other cases. Bring the whole puzzle together.

It might just be the breakthrough we were waiting for.

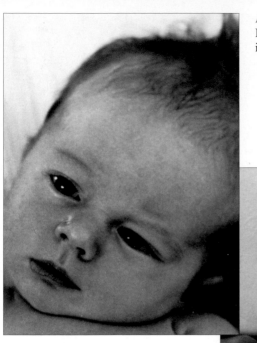

Left: My beautiful baby boy. Damien was born in Singapore in 1980.

Right: Damien looking up at his dad, with his sister, Sarah on the right.

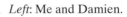

Left: Me and Damien.

Right: Damien looking very cute in his Mickey Mouse t-shirt.

Left: Damien (centre) with his brother, James and Sarah in 1988.

Left: Damien, at the age of 9.

Right: A treasured Christmas with all my children – Damien with James, Sarah and baby Melissa.

Left: Damien and his little sister, Melissa at home.

Right: Damien's school photo taken when he was 14.

Below: Damien and Ed relaxing together.

Above: Damien on one of his final birthdays with us.

Below: The final photo of Damien, that we found after he went missing.

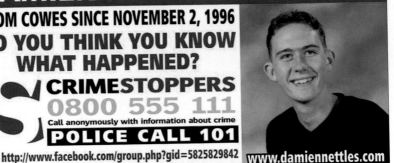

Two of the many appeal posters that we have produced in our efforts to find Damien over the years.

Above: Me with one of my treasured photos of Damien.

Left: An appeal poster produced by the Missing People charity, showing how Damien might look now.

missing

Can you help?

Damien Nettles
Age at disappearance: 16

Damien went missing on 2 November 1996 after a night out with friends on the Isle of Wight. Damien, who was living with his family in Gurnard at the time, was last seen shortly after midnight walking along the High Street in West Cowes.

He has not been seen or heard from since and his family and friends are frantically worried about him.

Damien is 6ft 3in tall, of slim build with brown hair and brown eyes.

The accompanying age-progressed image of Damien has been created by the charity Missing People to suggest how he might look now.

Fresh Appeal

W h e r e   i s   D a m i e n ?

As the 20th Anniversary of Damien's disappearance is approaching, we would appeal to the people of the Isle of Wight to come forward if you know or have heard where Damien's remains are buried. His family have suffered more than necessary and Damien deserves a dignified burial.

Missing since 2 November 1996

- White
- 6ft 3in tall
- Slim build
- Short brown hair shaved at the back
- Brown eyes

He was last seen wearing:

- Black fleece jacket
- Dark blue jeans
- Black boots

In recent weeks three historic missing cases have been resolved with fresh evidence coming to light. If it was your child, please consider how you would feel if he/she disappeared, never to be seen again. We would welcome any new intelligence.

Please sign the petition to provide Hampshire Police with funding to find Damien's remains

https://petition.parliament.uk/petitions/164442

Damien is featured in BBC3 series "Unsolved" – The Boy Who Disappeared

BBC3 iPlayer– Unsolved: http://www.bbc.co.uk/programmes/p041fkdp

BBC3 YouTube Unsolved: https://www.youtube.com/playlist?list=PL64ScZt2I7wEgGLbHcNCWvfHd9QPIV

It is a criminal offence to withhold information regarding a suspected murder
Perverting the Course of Justice & Preventing Lawful Burial of a Corpse

CRIMESTOPPERS Hampshire & Isle of Wight
Call 0800 555 111 or Hampshire Police on 101

http://www.facebobook.com/groups/damienrichardnettles @DamienNettles #DamienNettles

A fresh appeal for Damien. I'll never stop fighting for my baby boy.

All photographs © Valerie Nettles.

CHAPTER TEN

W E NEEDN'T HAVE GOT OUR HOPES UP. EVEN AFTER DAMIEN'S CASE was handed to the Major Crimes Unit, nothing much seemed to be happening that I was aware of. Almost a year passed with sparse communication from the police. If we did hear anything about the case, it wasn't from them. It was from people in the community or local reporters. In August 2002 a reporter from the *Isle of Wight County Press* called me.

'Do you know anything about this search at Branstone Cross?' she asked.

'What search?' I asked.

I had no idea what she was talking about, so she filled me in on what she'd heard. Apparently a massive search was under way in a cornfield in Branstone Cross. Twenty specialist officers were using high-tech ground-penetrating radars to search for a body. The search had been prompted by information provided by a man already in custody.

'It can't be Damien they're looking for,' I said, shaking with disbelief. 'They would have told me, surely?'

I was completely in the dark. And completely devastated. I sat by the phone and kept my eyes glued to news back on the island, compulsively checking my email in wait of some kind of update. Eventually, after a few days, I received an after-the-fact summary of the investigation from the police. They seemed a little surprised that I already knew about the search. But they still didn't seem to think there was anything wrong with the fact that they hadn't informed me about it in the first place.

It emerged that a prisoner who was on remand for sexual offences against children had claimed that he'd killed a fifteen-year-old child on the Isle of Wight in the mid-1990s. It was close enough to Damien's age for them to take action. He'd detailed Branstone Cross as the burial site but the search had been called off after three days when nothing was found. They believed the man had been lying. A few weeks later it was confirmed. He'd made up the whole story and could even be prosecuted for wasting police time.

Damien's story had been an easy one to latch on to. With all the rumour and speculation, his disappearance had practically become an urban myth. It worried me that fact was starting to blur with fiction, that the only recent new lead had been a lie. It also worried me that, with us no longer on the island, the facts about Damien's disappearance were falling from people's minds. I was concerned that Damien was being forgotten. I wanted people to remember him. I wanted people to carry on asking the question: *What happened to Damien Nettles?*

For me, life moved slowly and painfully forward. I knew that I appeared to be okay. I didn't even really cry any more – not in a way that anyone could see, anyway. I'd somehow mastered a silent sob, an internal cry that only I could feel and hear. Beneath my quiet façade there was turmoil, confusion. Grief tinged with anger, remorse and bitterness, and a constant acute feeling of loss. But I'd learned to hide it. Remain outwardly calm, inwardly screaming. I often found myself surprised that I was still alive, carrying on.

Well before he'd vanished, and always concerned about his vulnerability, I used to say to Damien: 'Be careful. I would die if anything was to happen to you.' I meant it. After he vanished, I didn't think I'd last a year.

But I did. I lasted a year.

Then another and another and another.

Now it was seven and a half years later and I was still standing. When I asked myself why, the answer was simple: I needed to know what had happened to my boy.

* * *

In the summer of 2003 we'd been alerted to some remains that had washed up on a beach in Swanage in Dorset. We'd been waiting for a call back from police after DNA testing had been concluded. When the results from DCI Williams came, he confirmed that it wasn't Damien. It was another missing boy, Daniel Nolan. He'd gone missing from Hamble in 2001 and I'd been in contact with his mother, Pauline, a few times through email. My heart broke for her, but at least her search was at an end. I felt some comfort in the fact that she'd be able to lay him to rest properly and grieve for her boy.

During the course of the call, Williams also mentioned some bones that had washed up near Warsash in southern Hampshire, around thirty kilometres from the Isle of Wight.

'Might they be Damien's?' I interjected.

'Oh no,' he said.

'How do you know?' I asked.

'He's the wrong height,' he said.

He described the discovery as the skeletal remains of a male aged between fourteen and sixteen, roughly 5ft 9ins in height. They'd been able to use something called isotope analysis to identify that the male came from Dorset, Hampshire or the Isle of Wight. It almost fitted Damien's profile.

I felt sick to my stomach. How could they not think there was a chance it could be him? The height was out, but the age and location . . . this could be Damien. Of all the poor souls who had washed up on rocks and beaches in the area, this was one of the closest matches. Who knew what toll the tide would take on fragile bones being tossed about, year after year, amongst the stones and shingle of the seabed?

I steeled myself for a battle. They *had* to check if it was Damien or not.

We went back and forth, Williams remaining adamant that it couldn't be him, and me arguing to the contrary. In the end I was left feeling like they didn't *want* to check. I pushed and pushed, refusing to back down.

'We need to check if this is Damien,' I insisted. 'Please could you check the DNA against the swab you took from me in 1996.'

In the end, he relented. 'Of course, Mrs Nettles,' he said. I knew DNA analysis took time, so I did my best to wait patiently. But when I still hadn't had an update by 23 October, I called back again.

'The forensic anthropologist hasn't come back to me,' Williams said. 'I'll chase it up.'

Not long after, I made another follow-up call. But instead of getting Williams, I spoke to a DI called John Murphy. He'd been mentioned before as being on the case but I hadn't had much to do with him. I pressed him for a wider update on Damien's investigation, to see what else was being done aside from the DNA analysis of the Warsash remains.

'We might have some news about the CCTV from Yorkies,' he said.

My ears pricked up. 'Go on,' I replied, clutching the receiver.

'We think we have identified one of the unknown men in the footage. We think he was a well-known drug dealer from the area.'

'Was?' I asked.

'Yes. He died last year,' he said. He didn't elaborate further or furnish me with a name. He wasn't allowed to.

'He was in there at the same time as Damien?' I asked, for clarification.

'We believe so,' he said.

Murphy explained how they were going to try and confirm the man's identity. I have to admit I found that a little odd. If he was such a well-known drug dealer, they must have had dealings with him before?

Surely they'd know if it was him or not?

But I let them get on with it. Assumed it was something that was required as part of procedure. I mentioned it to Ed and James in passing that evening over tea. James frowned and put his hand to his chin.

'I went to school with a couple of kids whose dad died last year,' he said. 'I wonder if there's any connection?'

Maybe it was simply a coincidence. I was now certain there

was more than one drug dealer on the island. But what if it wasn't? I decided to make contact with one of the reporters from the *County Press*. I'd learned that journalists were sometimes more aware of seedy goings-on on the island than the police. Maybe they could give me a name? I told the reporter what DI Murphy had said. Immediately she snapped her fingers.

'I bet it will be Nicky McNamara,' she said.

'Who?' I asked.

'Nicky McNamara,' she said. 'He wasn't a nice guy. He died last year.'

Turns out he was well known on the island – a nasty man with a violent temper and an addiction to heroin. His death had been drug-related and had happened under suspicious circumstances. It wasn't much, but it was something new to go on.

I struggled to make sense of it. Not that it made much sense. It baffled me that this man was being in any way linked to my son's disappearance. Even if this Nicky McNamara character had been in Yorkies at the same time as Damien, what was the connection between the two? Nothing in the CCTV footage I had seen showed an altercation or even a wrong look exchanged. If something had happened after they left Yorkies, then surely Damien wouldn't have looked so at ease walking home with his chips at 12:02am?

If Damien wanted a bit of weed, he could probably have asked a friend – someone who had an older brother or sister who knew someone who could get some. He wouldn't approach a complete stranger. I wrestled with the possibilities. No matter which way I looked at it, it didn't make sense.

Between that unfolding story and the worry of the Warsash

VALERIE NETTLES

remains I was a mess – unable to sleep or think straight until word came back from the police about the CCTV footage. It wasn't the dealer they had thought it was. They still didn't give me his name, but I knew it from my own sources now. Truth be told, I felt more and more like a detective myself every day. I shared Nicky McNamara's name with my family and James recognised it immediately.

'I *do* know his sons,' he gasped. 'I even went to his house once.'

'You did what?' I gasped.

'I went round to Nicky's house with a friend from school who knew his sons,' he said. 'Nicky was there. It was after Damien disappeared.'

My stomach lurched and I brought my hand to my mouth in shock. One of my children had been in the home of a known drug dealer. One who might have had something to do with Damien's disappearance to boot.

'What happened when you were there?' I asked.

'I did think he was a bit weird,' he said. 'He asked who we were. When they said I was Damien Nettles's brother . . .' James trailed off.

'What did he do?' I urged.

'He just flipped,' he said, finally. 'Told them to get me out of the house.'

James had not thought much of it at the time. His mate had just told him that Nicky was a bit of a dodgy guy, acting that way.

But maybe it was something more?

Was he the 'who' in one of the horror stories we'd heard over the years? In every incident and rumour that cropped up, we looked hard for some relevance.

James later confided that Nicky's kids would taunt him if they saw him out, shouting across the street: 'What do you call fish bait? Damien!' He hadn't told me at the time because he didn't want to upset me. There was more to come too. Melissa piped up. It turned out Nicky's daughter was in the year above her at school.

'She suddenly started asking me lots of questions about what the police were saying about Damien,' she said. 'I wondered why.'

Again, it could be a coincidence. But what if it wasn't? Time pressed on. Although the police didn't give me a name, they did tell me whom they had asked to ID McNamara.

'We showed the footage to the man's family and they said it wasn't him,' Murphy said.

I was left speechless on the other end of the phone.

They asked his family?

Of course they'd say it wasn't him! A known drug dealer, spotted in the vicinity of a missing person, just before he'd vanished off the face of the earth? *In suspicious circumstances.* They were hardly going to grass him up, were they? Even if he was dead.

Despite the confusing information I had around Nicky McNamara, everything paled into insignificance as I waited for the result of the DNA tests on the remains from Warsash. Thanksgiving came and went and Christmas was around the corner yet again. Celebrations were always hard without Damien, but the uncertainty around the remains crushed any spark of joy or fun. My stomach was in knots and I barely ate or slept. By early December I couldn't take it any more. I wanted the results to come before Christmas. I emailed DCI Williams, filled with desperation. I wanted to catch him before he took leave over the Christmas break with his family. He responded via email.

'I apologise for not resolving this earlier. We have been waiting on the Forensic Science Service to try and develop a nuclear DNA profile from the bones but they have failed to do this,' the email read.

My heart sank into my stomach as I continued reading. 'They have managed to extract maternal-line DNA known as mitochondrial DNA.' This was a type of DNA passed on almost exclusively from mother to child through the egg cell. In order to test for it, they needed a new swab from me.

They might still get some answers.

DCI Williams said they would pay for a kit to be sent to me. I just needed to arrange for my doctor to take the swab, to make sure it was done properly. Once they had it, they would be able to compare my maternal DNA against the DNA from the bones. I replied and agreed, asking them to send the kit to me. They responded to say the testing kit would soon be on its way.

A week passed, then another. The kit didn't turn up. By February I was so incensed that I mentioned it to a reporter on the *County Press*.

'I feel angry, let down and disappointed,' I said. 'I just do not know how it can take so long to put a kit in the post to me.' They once again challenged the police on my behalf, asking them what was taking so long. Almost immediately the kit turned up, shortly followed by a phone call from DCI Williams, offering a profuse apology. Days later a friend emailed me an article from the *County Press*: APOLOGY TO MUM OF MISSING TEENAGER.

The story explained about how long I'd waited for the DNA kit. DCI Williams was quoted in the article, explaining how Damien's case had been looked after by the Major Crime Department since 2002, and how potential burial sites had been excavated. One line in his comment jumped out at me: 'The department remains committed in its resolve to pursue any reasonable line of enquiry.'

How could I trust what they judged to be a 'reasonable' line of enquiry? I'd had to fight tooth and nail to get them to DNA test the remains of a young male from the South whose profile was similar to Damien's. If that wasn't 'reasonable' then what was? Truth be told, if the local paper hadn't got involved, I don't know if I would have ever received the kit.

On 27 February, finally with the kit in my hands, I went to my doctor. She took the swab and sent it straight back to Hampshire Constabulary for analysis. They received it on 1 March. As simple as that. A few days.

Not months!

Again I had to play the waiting game, checking my emails anxiously every day for news from the police. After a few days, an email did appear. But it wasn't from the police and it wasn't about the DNA. It was from Corran. She'd received some information. A lady by the name of Lynn Hammond had contacted her saying she had reason to believe that Damien and another boy had been taken to a chalet owned by two paedophiles, down on Gurnard Marsh. She claimed they had abused both boys, killed Damien, then wrapped him in a carpet and burned his body in a blue car.

They'd got the other boy to help them do the dirty work.

As I continued reading, my stomach churned. She'd even

highlighted potential gravesites. It was such a detailed account. There must at least be a foundation of truth in it? Then I saw it. The name of the other boy – *Harry Corbett*.

It took a moment before I realised why the name was familiar. Then I remembered. It was the same name that the nurse had given to us back in 1998! I immediately followed up with the police. But Murphy brushed it off, acted like he'd already heard it all before.

'She's obsessed with paedophiles, that one,' he said about Lynn. 'And the lad's an addict. Completely unreliable.' I was baffled by his dismissiveness.

'There's no evidence that Damien was murdered anyway,' he said, trying to placate me.

But there was no proof he wasn't, either. Had they even looked into this theory? And if so, why was I only finding it out now, from a local, rather than the police?

In light of DI Murphy's comments, I did some research on Lynn. She was a town councillor, which suggested she was a source worth considering. She wasn't some druggie that couldn't be trusted; she was an upstanding member of the community. Apparently, though, years earlier, Lynn had openly spoken out against the housing of paedophiles in halfway houses in Cowes. I gasped as I realised: I *had* heard about Lynn before. She'd been involved in the news story that had prompted me to ask police if they thought paedophiles might be responsible for Damien's disappearance. Back then they'd said Damien would have been 'too old' to be of interest to them. Could they have been mistaken?

I could barely think straight. So many fragments of gossip and speculation were starting to morph into a bigger picture.

But a picture with huge gaps and no real evidence, much like all the other rumour and speculation that surrounded the case.

Whatever information I gave, however I asked for help, I was always left waiting. Two weeks after sending the DNA samples, I emailed to see if there was any news. While I had reason to be in touch, I took the opportunity to share the snippet of information about the paedophiles from Lynn, which Corran had included in her email to me. I asked what was being done with the information.

Again I waited. And waited. But I received no reply. Nothing, until 30 March. That morning, an email from Hampshire Constabulary popped up in my inbox: *DNA Results*.

Finally. My whole body was shaking as I clicked 'open'. I could barely bring myself to look. When I finally did, I heaved a sigh of relief. The test had proved negative as a match. It wasn't Damien. The police had been correct, but actually *knowing* emphatically and without doubt put my mind at ease. Then, as always, the relief gave way to despair. We were now over seven years without an answer. Any explanation for why our beautiful boy had vanished from our lives.

Into thin air . . .

When would we get the answers that we so desperately needed, that we deserved?

This life, suspended between grief and fear, held down by the weight of the unknown, was good for no one.

Infuriatingly, the email contained no reference to my question about the information from Lynn. I replied straight back, asking for them to respond to that question too. Williams's response was swift and curt:

'I take John Murphy's point that there is no evidence that

Damien was murdered, but of course conversely there is no evidence that he was not. Damien's disappearance remains unexplained so we will continue to keep our options open, and consider and explore information received.'

What kind of explanation was that? And why were they still skirting around the information from Lynn that I'd shared with them? Yet another statement fobbed off and deemed irrelevant, this time because they considered Lynn to be 'obsessed' with paedophiles. How could they let such opinions cloud the investigation?

Again we were at an impasse. Frustration took hold of me. Despite all the promises made in the meeting we'd had with DI Stewart, before we'd moved to the States; despite the odd flurry of activity, usually prompted by us pushing, it felt like nothing was happening on Damien's case. Even when there was new information!

We just couldn't get a break.

So we made a decision. We'd make it easy for people to come to us directly with information. We were complete novices but we somehow managed to set up a website for Damien. It contained photos and all the information we had about his disappearance, along with a simple contact form. We decided to be proactive in this new world of the missing, sharing information about other missing people too. We knew how much support families like us needed.

We told people we knew about it and asked them to share it far and wide. As we did, friends and acquaintances suggested that I also set up a Facebook page for myself. I'd never heard of it before, but apparently Facebook had started out as a way for university students to share pictures and updates about what they were doing with friends. You could even send messages within the program, kind of like an email. I couldn't see any harm in trying so, with the help of the kids, I set up an account in my name and made 'friends' with people I knew who were on it. I connected with other families of the missing and we shared pictures and information about our loved ones. It was all quite nifty and very easy to use. In a way, it gave me a new lease of life – a way by which I could communicate with people about Damien without the police in the middle.

People from the island began to reach out to me via my Facebook page. Some were quick to share information with me but refused to go to the police, rendering the information as little more than useless gossip. In many other cases, though, people just wanted to connect. That told me something: people still thought about Damien.

People still wondered, as we did, what had happened to him. I was going to do my best to keep that spark of interest alive. I even booked a flight back to the UK, so I could once again pound the pavement and speak to anyone who would listen.

Soon, our new lines of communication delivered a lead – an email from the family of a sixteen-year-old boy called George Mortimer, who had been murdered in 1999 by a paedophile called Darren Collings. It was a horrific story. So too was the information they shared with us. Their investigation had found a link between Collings and the Isle of Wight. They'd shared the information with police at the time, but they had no idea what had been done with it. They'd felt compelled to contact us directly.

My stomach churned as I learned what happened to poor George. Collings had battered him to death with a hammer before sexually abusing him. I could barely bring myself to consider the thought of my boy meeting the same fate. But the information begged the question: could Collings have been around when Damien disappeared? If he HAD been on the island, perhaps he might have been one of the paedophiles Lynn had mentioned? It was an angle I would have to pursue.

CHAPTER ELEVEN

Ahead of my trip back to the island, I liaised with National Missing Persons Helpline to arrange some media interviews. They even provided me with a digitally enhanced age-progression photograph that showed what Damien would look like eight years on from his disappearance, created using photos of his male family members.

The image tore at every one of my heartstrings. Technology had transformed the boy who'd left our house that evening into a man. His childlike features had been replaced by a stronger jawline and brow, but I could still see my little boy in those twinkling eyes. He was so handsome. Of course, by now, more than just his face would have changed. At twenty-three, he'd have finished university. Was this what he might have looked like in his graduation photograph? Would he now have a job, working as a marine biologist? Or would he have decided to travel the world before settling down into a career?

I would have given anything to have those answers – to have seen that transformation happening in front of me. Instead, we could only imagine what he might have made of his life.

I included the images in my leaflets and posters. I was on a mission to remind people that we were still here. That Damien was still missing and that we still needed help and information. All I wanted was to jog someone's memory or appeal to someone's conscience. To know what had become of my son.

While the information about the paedophiles on the island was concerning and compelling, there were two things I was really focused on finding new information about: the alleged sighting of Damien on Baring Road, at what would have been 12:30am on Sunday 3 November 1996, and the other unidentified men in the chip shop. They chatted amongst themselves and came and went in a group. What might they be able to tell us? I knew that anything new on either of these things could completely revitalise the case. They may have seen or heard something, or recognised one of the other men as the local drug dealer rumoured to be in there – contrary to his family's statements. In fact, they might be the only things that could keep it alive.

National Missing Persons Helpline arranged for a production company to film me on the island for a documentary about Damien. I was also scheduled to appear on GMTV, as we reached the eighth anniversary of his disappearance. As part of the feature, I would be able to make an appeal for information about the men in Yorkies. I also arranged to meet DCI Williams for an update on the case. Everything was set. I was prepped and focused. Then, in early November, the phone rang. It was a reporter called Stephanie Marsh, from *The Times*.

It wasn't unusual to receive calls like this from reporters around the anniversary of Damien's disappearance. In fact, it was more unusual for it *not* to happen. I didn't mind. I welcomed anything that kept Damien in the public eye. She asked me about the case and I explained that I was heading back to the Isle of Wight in a few weeks' time, to try and generate some new leads. I told her we were still none the wiser as to what had happened to Damien.

'I have nothing to go on, only different parts of a jigsaw puzzle and no picture,' I said. 'My thought is that someone on the island must know something. After all this time we need closure. I can't let go.' I meant every word. Someone on the island knew something, they just weren't telling us. I hadn't realised just how close to home it might be.

A few days later, Stephanie's story was published. When I saw the headline I was confused, surprised and completely dismayed: ISLAND BOY ANNOYED DRUG SELLER ON THE DAY HE VANISHED.

My heart was in my throat as I read the article. Some of Damien's 'former friends' had apparently spoken to the journalist and claimed that he was the victim of a 'botched drug attack'. Two of these people were unnamed, including a man in his early twenties. But there was one very familiar name mentioned in the piece: Alex Roberts – Damien's former bandmate and close friend.

The article claimed that it was 'common knowledge' among young people on the island that foul play was to blame for my son's sudden and unexpected disappearance. The unnamed man, who did not want to be identified, told the reporter that Damien had angered a local drug dealer shortly after leaving

Yorkies chip shop, with fatal consequences. Although he wasn't quoted directly, the paper also claimed Alex had said that many people involved in the drug scene in Cowes in the late 1990s were well aware of Damien's fate, and urged them to speak out.

The article also cited an account claiming that Damien's body had been moved in the back of a car. These were the same accounts we'd heard and shared with police over the years, only to be told they weren't credible – yet *The Times* had been confident enough to publish them. Williams was also quoted in the article, highlighting the unidentified men in the chip shop as 'one of the most significant potential leads'.

It didn't take me long to figure out whom the other boys that Stephanie had spoken to were. I understood why they wanted to remain anonymous and I commended them for speaking out. What I didn't understand was why they hadn't done it sooner. They could have told the police, or even me. That same day, as I mulled over the article and what it meant for Damien's case, I received an email from Williams. It read:

'I am quite frankly disappointed with the article, which in my view was not balanced and suggested that Damien's friends knew of an argument with a drug dealer.' He explained that none of the statements given by sixty or so friends and acquaintances of Damien's had suggested anything of the sort. So why would they say it? What did they have to gain from lying? It was reassuring to hear from the police that the news report was not balanced, but it left me in another quandary.

Was he referring to statements taken back in 1996 or more recently? Maybe they felt they weren't being listened to by police and spoke to the media instead? Maybe they had been scared then but weren't anymore? Nicky McNamara was dead now, after all, along with a number of his associates, I'd heard. Or was what the boys told *The Times* a compilation of the Chinese whispers and gossip they'd heard circulating the Isle of Wight about what happened to Damien?

The email even referenced the line of enquiry regarding McNamara, and how Murphy had personally interviewed anyone connected with that rumour, with no evidence to support it having yet been found. Then he told me that he was going to contact the journalist and ask her to reveal her sources. As if a reporter would do that!

I was overwhelmed with frustration. As with all of the leads that I believed would take us somewhere, the police didn't give this one any credence. My hopes were dashed yet again.

The whole gist of his email was that he didn't place much significance on the contents of the story at all. What's more, there was so much in the newspaper report I felt they blithely assumed I knew – things that had never been communicated to me by police, such as the suggestion that Damien had taken amphetamines. I knew about the pot, but nothing more.

Who had said this? And moreover, how had police verified the claim, with Damien not around to tell his side of the story? And as for Alex and these other friends of Damien's, why had they never said these things to my face? When I returned to England, I intended to find out.

* * *

A few days before my flight I'd received another email about the paedophile connection. This time it was directly from Lynn. She'd seen the story in *The Times* and heard how the boys' claims had been dismissed, just like hers. She was angry and didn't understand why so many pieces of information were seemingly being ignored or disregarded. I felt her rage and fully intended to share my feelings with Williams at our meeting. The production company had requested to film it for the *Missing* programme, which was due to be broadcast the following year, but Hampshire Constabulary had refused. They instead agreed to allow a mocked-up meeting to be filmed, covering agreed topics, after the official meeting had taken place.

I understood that they wouldn't want to discuss operational information with the media, but this could have been worked around. I wondered why they were so cagey.

What didn't they want people to see?

The 'real' meeting took place at Cowes Police Station. I took two friends with me for moral support: Fiona Prentice, a magistrate who was a friend from way back, and Tim Blackman, whom I'd met through mutual friends from the island. Tim was the father of Lucie Blackman, who had gone missing in Tokyo in 2000. Tragically, seven months after her disappearance, her body was found. The trial of the man accused of her murder was still ongoing.

The meeting was like any other update meeting I'd had. DCI Williams was there, along with DI Murphy, the man who'd first brought Nicky McNamara to my attention, even if not by name. We went through all the usual confirmation that new information had been followed up and they were still seeking new leads. *The Times* article didn't get much of a mention. It was all the 'same old, same old'. Until I asked a question.

'What about Nicky McNamara?' From that moment, things took an odd turn.

'Pardon?' Williams asked, appearing startled.

'The drug dealer that I was informed may have been connected to the case. The one who recently died of a drug overdose,' I clarified.

'I don't know what you're talking about, Mrs Nettles,' Williams responded. I shot a look at Murphy. It was him I'd had this conversation with. He averted his eyes and my blood boiled.

'I was told by an officer in 2003 that a local drug dealer was believed to be in that CCTV footage in Yorkies. That it was being investigated,' I said, boring holes into Murphy's head. He just sat silently with his head down.

'I'm sorry, Mrs Nettles,' Williams said again. 'I think you must be mistaken. I don't know where this is coming from or why you make that connection.'

From your officer here! I thought. *From our email correspondence earlier this month.*

But I bit my lip. I was mystified by the direction of the conversation, not to mention a little intimidated. Despite everything that had happened, I still hadn't grown used to being in police stations or the processes involved in liaising with officers. In the end, Fiona spoke.

'Oh well, it looks like someone is confused here,' she said.

I was taken aback by her comment and hoped she didn't think it was me that was confused. But I understood how it looked. Murphy and Williams had really pulled the rug from beneath my feet. Even worse, they were not giving me the answers I was desperate to hear about Nicky McNamara. I'd thought we were getting somewhere, making progress. But Murphy didn't even bother to look up at me for the rest of the interview. In the end, I relented, bemused by the whole conversation and unwilling to be made to look any more of a fool.

The meeting eventually concluded. The overarching feedback from the police was that they'd exhausted all reasonable lines of enquiry and drawn no new conclusions. It was devastating. While they told me that the case was still ongoing, while they promised me that certain leads were still being 'bottomed out', it felt like they were giving up.

What about the paedophile theory?

What about the men in Yorkies who still hadn't been identified?

Why weren't they fighting tooth and nail to find out?

After the meeting I had very little to say. I was disappointed and embarrassed that both officers had acted like they'd never heard of Nicky McNamara. I was concerned that both Tim and Fiona would think I had it wrong. For the rest of the day I was mentally reeling. The events of the meeting gnawed at my brain. This whole case was now eight years old. I carried eight years of conversations and snippets of information in my head. Had I been mistaken? Had I confused the information? Had I stitched facts together with fragments of gossip and hearsay? *NO!* I told myself, shaking away any creeping self-doubt. I was sure. I was absolutely certain that both officers had made reference to McNamara when communicating with me.

When I got back to my brother Nigel's house in Gloucester, I went through my emails and searched through all of my correspondence with Williams and Murphy. There it was, plain as day, from a few weeks earlier. Williams had mentioned the investigation into rumours relating to Nicky McNamara and some of his associates. I even found emails to Sarah referencing McNamara too.

I collated all the emails and sent them straight to DCI Williams, highlighting the embarrassment he had caused me at the meeting that day. He replied a couple of days later, offering apologies. He claimed that he must have forgotten the interaction. How could the lead investigator on my son's case forget conversations he'd had with me and my family about key pieces of evidence? About potential suspects? The lack of communication and constant miscommunication was unforgivable. The families of other missing people I'd met all seemed to have Family Liaison Officers in place to manage these relationships. I hadn't the faintest idea why I didn't have one. God knows we needed it!

Truth was, they'd let us down from the day that Damien had vanished. No matter how many new faces joined the investigation, they always fell short of even mediocre communication. I was beginning to wonder how much more I could take.

Before I left the island, I tried to contact Alex about the article in *The Times*. If he'd been willing to open up to Stephanie, maybe he would be able to tell me more. I called his mother, who had at one time been a good friend, as a starting point.

'Do you think I could speak to Alex about the newspaper story?' I asked.

She wasn't receptive. In fact, she was upset and exasperated that Alex had said anything of the sort to a reporter. He'd moved away, but his younger brother still lived in town. It was as if she felt he'd somehow put him at risk.

What was it that people were still scared of?

'I'll give him your number and ask him if he wants to talk to you,' she said.

But I never heard back.

* * *

I returned to the USA physically and emotionally exhausted. I did my best to stay on top of the police, but I rarely got a response. Everywhere I turned I was hitting brick walls. Just before I'd left, the *County Press*, as supportive as ever, had published another appeal for information, focusing on the possible sighting of Damien on Baring Road at 12:30am on Sunday 3 November 1996. Despite that, the police went silent. It was like they'd washed their hands of me, of Damien, of our whole family, in fact. I felt like we were a thorn in their sides.

My heart would leap when an email came in from one of the investigators on the case, only to be disappointed to read that it was just an apology for not getting back to me sooner.

They'd been 'busy working on a murder case', apparently. Well, what was Damien's, then?

Maybe there was no evidence to prove foul play yet, but wasn't that their job? To go out and find it?

Months passed with nothing until March 2005, when I was informed in a 'confidential' email that the police would be carrying out a six- to eight-week investigation around Nicky McNamara's associates. They told me I wasn't to speak about this to anyone, and that for this period of time they would be incommunicado.

At last! We were all buoyed with hope. Had they actually finally pulled their finger out? Taken heed of what was being said around town? Had something come out of that article in

The Times? Whatever it was, I was just happy that something tangible seemed to be happening. Perhaps now some light could be shed on who this man was and what his relevance might be to this investigation.

I told only our little family unit: Ed, Sarah, Melissa and James. I knew that mentioning it to any friends on the island could put the investigation at risk, so I kept schtum.

Eight weeks passed, but we heard nothing. Well, they did say they'd be incommunicado. We allowed for the investigation starting after we received the email and possibly overrunning a little. They may have needed more time, after all. But May turned to June. There was still nothing. I was at my wits' end. A bag of nerves, living on a few hours' sleep each night as I waited for news. Eventually Sarah cracked.

'This is outrageous. Look at the state you're in,' she said. 'They're trying to keep you quiet and they're doing nothing fast!'

She was right. While I knew there was plenty of operational detail they couldn't share with me, the complete failure to communicate at all left me feeling like they were pushing us into silence, in the hope that maybe – just maybe – we'd go away. In the end, I sent an email to Williams. It was short, but told him exactly how I was feeling and what I planned to do next.

'I am feeling pretty well abandoned at this point and am working on the assumption that there IS nothing happening regarding my son's case or anything related since I have not had any reply to several emails that I have sent recently asking for updates,' I wrote. 'Working on this assumption, I feel free to discuss whatever I may with anyone who will listen.'

To my amazement, after the weeks of silence, an email from Williams dropped into my inbox a few hours later. My jaw swung open as I read its contents.

'Valerie, I am sorry that we the police have not met the high standard of communication demanded by yourself,' it began. He went on to claim that work was continuing on Damien's case, and that he'd even increased the size of the investigation team to three. He made a point of saying he didn't intend to discuss the specific detail of the information with me, something that I of course understood. I didn't want detail, just reassurance: an email or call to say, 'We're still on the case.'

The whole email oozed the same dismissiveness I'd felt when I first reported Damien missing – *crazy, hysterical, demanding woman.* But it was one paragraph that felt like a knife to my heart:

'The investigation is one of fifty or so being investigated at any one time by the Major Crime Department with finite resources,' Williams said. 'This case does not carry the priority of current homicide investigations, stranger rapes, crimes in action where life is at risk.'

In other words, your son doesn't matter that much. I read on, tears pricking my eyes and my hands clenched in rage. It was insulting to Damien and that hurt me to my very core.

'I confidently predict that Damien's unexplained disappearance has received more police time than in the history of any other missing person from the Hampshire and Isle of Wight area,' he concluded.

Was I supposed to be grateful? Most of the case was made up of information we had sourced, not the police. Nine years on we were still none the wiser and he sounded like he wanted a pat on the back! It was the very last thing he would be getting from me or any of my family after that email. I was sick to death of feeling like a burden, fed up of seeing Damien's case being treated as unimportant. I was bewildered and tired. But most of all, I was done with Hampshire Police. My fear of challenging them began to dissipate. If Williams's last email had set cogs turning in my brain about the way we were being treated, it was one received three months later that launched me into action.

On 7 September 2005, four months after the investigation into Nicky McNamara was supposed to have taken place, Williams emailed with an update on the investigation. It contained nothing of real note, apart from the closing lines.

'I am taking some leave in the Alps during the next couple of weeks (sarcastic comments not invited. I have worked throughout the summer), I will update you further upon my return,' the email read.

My jaw hit the floor. His tone stung. I know I had pushed them, challenged them on the standard of their communications. This had clearly put a strain on our relationship, but for him to speak to me like this – I shook my head in disbelief. Did he know what I would give to have a normal life? One where I could forget the world and take a trip somewhere nice? I hadn't asked for this. All I had ever asked – right from day one – was that the police do everything that they could to help find my son.

Do it when it should have been done. In the way it should have been done.

But they never had.

I was convinced that mistakes they had made, testimonies

they had dismissed as 'unreliable', had all led to Damien's case still not being solved. I was left wondering how many other things had been missed. Even my caseworker from National Missing Persons Helpline was unable to reach Williams, which supported my feeling that Damien was very low on the police priority list. I knew they'd treated my family and me in an appalling manner and I'd finally reached my breaking point.

It stopped now.

CHAPTER TWELVE

I T WASN'T JUST THE PERSONAL HURT — THE ALL-CONSUMING disappointment every time another line of enquiry we put forward was disregarded. It wasn't just the pain of being no closer to finding Damien. It was more than that. The more I learned about the workings of the law and missing person cases – in many instances through the National Missing Persons Helpline – the more I realised how much had been done wrong. Right from the start.

Vital opportunities had been missed; chances to find out what had happened to my son. Poor attitude and incompetence had deprived us of answers. Of any kind of resolution.

That first day – when I had turned to my local police force, when I had arrived on the steps of Cowes Police Station in tears and terrified for the wellbeing of my sixteen-year-old son – I had no idea what was meant to happen next.

Why would I? No one expects to find themselves in that situation. No one prepares themselves for what to do if their child goes missing. Everything I knew about missing person cases at that point was drawn from what I had seen on television or read in the news. My expectation was that news of a missing child would have the police out in droves, airborne searches, rescue dogs and sombre press conferences. That didn't happen for Damien. And it should have.

At first I'd been naive and perhaps a little intimidated by having to deal with the police. I'd thought my expectations had been wrong, skewed by sensational media stories. But then the mistakes started. Clear failure in just doing the basics of the job:

- Getting Damien's age wrong.
- Picking out the wrong person in video footage.
- Cherry-picking the leads they did or didn't follow based on their opinions.
- Losing vital CCTV evidence.

I'd looked into the responsibilities of the police in criminal investigations and tried to ascertain exactly what we should have expected. One extract from the Criminal Procedure and Investigations Act 1996 set alarm bells ringing in my head: 'Any police officer involved in the investigation into alleged crimes has a duty to record and retain material which may be relevant to the investigation'.

It didn't say anything about officers deciding what was or wasn't relevant. It didn't give them the right to choose. It didn't brush off the loss of evidence like they had with the CCTV footage. For almost nine years, Hampshire Constabulary had met us with resistance. We'd had to fight for action every step of the way. In many cases we'd had to act as detectives ourselves.

A huge proportion of the information the police had in their hands was provided by us – by our supporters and friends of Damien. When the police *had* acted on their own volition, their communication with our family had been poor at best. It had caused us anguish and distress. More pain. How was any of this right? After almost a decade of fighting to keep my son's case alive, I knew I had to take the police to task. Complain about how the case had been handled and demand that the investigation into his disappearance be completely reviewed. Not by another officer from the force but by an external body – the Independent Police Complaints Commission.

It wasn't a personal attack on many of the officers on the case – Williams, Clarke or even poor Evans, who herself had been spectacularly let down by the force. It was about procedure, due care and the police's responsibility to those who found themselves in their care. In my heart I knew that Hampshire Constabulary had failed in their duty. To Damien, to me, to our family and our whole community.

Sitting at my computer, I took a deep breath. I'd been spurred on to this point by frustration and disappointment; by the pleas of my family who felt just as dismissed and poorly treated as I did. Now I needed to be calm and collected. I needed to channel that anger and emotion. I was surrounded by piles of newspaper cuttings and printouts of emails that had gone back and forth between me and Hampshire Police documenting every step of the journey that had brought us to this point. I looked around, then began typing, determined to ensure that my son's case would receive the care it needed. The care it had always deserved.

I started the letter: 'I would like to make a formal complaint regarding the investigation into my son, Damien Nettles's, case. I have, over the past eight, nearly nine years, been given assurances that certain information would be "bottomed out", and I would be given the feedback regarding these instances. This has, in several areas, not been forthcoming.'

I tried to be fair, explaining how I understood there were constraints on police time; that I knew there were other new and serious cases opening daily. But I also made it clear that I didn't believe Damien's case was being given the best possible care and attention.

And that I thought it had been mismanaged from the very start. I asked that a neighbouring police department, outside of Hampshire Constabulary, audit Damien's case to see where things had gone wrong. As well as getting answers for us, I really did believe it would help DCI Williams and his team. They'd only taken the investigation over in the last four years. They'd inherited a flawed case.

In the letter I questioned all the things I considered to be an issue: the initial lack of interest in the first few days by Cowes Police and the poor attitude of officers towards us; the slow response by the uniformed police and lethargic response from detectives in the first weeks after Damien disappeared. Then there was the information provided by Simon W in the days after Damien vanished, that he had been seen on Baring Road. Information the police discarded, as they considered him 'unreliable'. It was the same information they decided to act on fourteen months later. Why had they tried to pass this off to me as 'new evidence', and why didn't they act on it in the first place?

I covered the lost CCTV footage, the poor response to rumours of a local drug dealer's connection to Damien's disappearance, and DCI Williams's 'blank' about this whole part of the case when I'd attended the catch-up meeting with Tim and Fiona.

I explained how, since returning home after making that visit to the Isle of Wight, I'd been contacted by the police saying they were actively investigating individuals surrounding this drug dealer, and that they'd asked me to refrain from speaking about this to anyone on the island. Then I'd heard nothing for months on end, despite emails begging for information. Despite promises they would 'be in touch', there was nothing. As I reached the end of the letter, I finally let my feelings spill out onto the page. The words were raw and honest, pouring like blood from a fresh wound.

'It is cruel to be kept in such a state of limbo after so long,' I typed. 'I think the police have lost sight of the fact that, as his mother, I am extremely distraught at this time and sick with foreboding. I am desperate for closure. Agonising is the closest word I can come up with to describe this.' It was an old case to them, but the pain of Damien's disappearance was as fresh and raw to us today as it was the first day. It never eased.

'This is not acceptable treatment of my family,' I continued. 'I am being urged by them to take this step, as their confidence in this ongoing investigation is seriously undermined. My family believes I am effectively being kept quiet from further publicity by use of the fear that I might compromise my son's case if I say anything.'

Finally, I concluded: 'I am respectfully asking that a full investigation be made into my son's case from day one to the present by an independent police force from another county, please.'

* * *

I submitted the letter to the IPCC on 16 October 2005. I knew full well that the action of making a formal complaint would likely cause an even further breakdown of the relationship between our family and DCI Williams and his team. But the relationship that existed was already so damaged, so fragile, that it didn't seem to matter anymore. If it would get fresh eyes on the case, it was worth the risk. I soon had my response.

I was informed that the case would be fully reviewed but it would be by an officer from within Hampshire Constabulary. It wasn't exactly what I'd hoped for. I'd hoped that the case would be handed to the Metropolitan Police, or maybe even a force from up north. But at least this would bring some new blood to the case.

In February 2006 DCI Williams emailed to let me know that a review would be undertaken by a Detective Chief Inspector named David Kilbride. I was told that he was a well-regarded Senior Investigating Officer with a great deal of experience. He was highly respected in Hampshire Constabulary and Williams reassured me that he would consider every concern that I had raised. I had no choice but to put my trust in him.

Williams also told me that he was moving on. He felt he had exhausted all of his options on the case and intended to invite DCI Kilbride to appoint a new SIO to take over.

Fresh eyes!

The idea suited me fine. I didn't want someone who had clearly given up leading the investigation into my son's disappearance. I wanted someone who would fight for it.

As time moved on, we learned that DCI Kilbride was personally reviewing every single piece of documentation on the case. The report was to concentrate on the handling of three key areas: the sequence of events on the night that Damien went missing; the CCTV footage from Yorkies, and the intelligence and rumours that had circulated suggesting reasons not just for Damien's disappearance, but also his possible death.

All areas we felt had not been dealt with correctly.

I prayed that it would draw some new conclusions, even elevate the investigation from a missing person case to a suspected murder case. I knew the answers weren't going to come quickly, but at least I knew that something was happening.

Over the next twelve months, a trickle of communication continued between the police and our family. Some was from the IPCC and the Professional Standards Department with regards to the complaint, as well as some operational updates from Williams. As we waited for the outcome of the review, I became even more sensitive to new missing persons cases. I didn't enjoy holding the police to account, but the more I saw of other cases, the more certain I was that we had been let down. In May 2007 a story broke that perfectly underlined all of my concerns.

A toddler named Madeleine McCann had vanished from the apartment in which her family had been staying in Praia da Luz, a holiday resort in Portugal's Algarve. She and her two-year-old twin siblings had been left asleep in the ground-floor apartment while their parents, Kate and Gerry, dined in a restaurant fifty-five metres away.

The news coverage was blanket. My heart broke for Madeleine's parents as they addressed national and international media in a press conference that was arranged just days after the tot had vanished.

'Please do not scare her,' Kate begged, pain etched across her face. 'Please let us know where to find Madeleine or put her in a place of safety.'

I knew that feeling all too well. I still felt it to that day. It had never, ever left me. Seeing two parents desperate to find their loved and vulnerable child made me ache deep inside. I ached in empathy. But I ached for another reason too – for the fact we had never had that kind of exposure for Damien. That immediate response.

Within weeks there were reconstructions and a special edition of BBC's *Crimewatch* dedicated to finding Madeleine. There were more press conferences and endless police searches conducted by both Portuguese and British police forces. They were throwing everything at the case.

Why hadn't my Damien warranted the same response?

It wasn't the first time I'd felt that way, but it was a fresh reminder of how we'd been on the back foot since day one. All because the Isle of Wight police didn't do their job.

Coincidentally, a few days later, I received an update from Williams on Kilbride's review. There had been a meeting attended by Williams, Kilbride, the force's Head of CID, Ray Webb, and Superintendent Pat Ogden, from the Professional Standards Department. The report had been completed as they were appointing a new team to action its recommendations. What's more, we were asked to provide a date when Kilbride could come to visit us in Dallas to go through his findings with us in person.

It was a huge surprise – a senior officer, coming to us to discuss Damien's case. After everything we'd been through, it finally felt like we mattered. That Damien mattered and that something was going to get done.

CHAPTER THIRTEEN

D CI KILBRIDE WAS A SMART, FRIENDLY-LOOKING MAN, INCREDIBLY formal, as you might expect, and as polite as they came. When he travelled to America in July 2007, Ed and I invited him into our home. We sat with him around our kitchen table, each holding a copy of the extensive report. He read through every page and explained his approach to each section of the review.

As he spoke, I scribbled notes in the margins. Some of the timings didn't seem quite right, and I'd noted some conflicting information, but it was thorough and they had examined all of the areas I had asked them to. The read-through took almost four hours. There were no names in the report, just police identification codes. My mind boggled as I tried to work out who was who, as I knew that Kilbride wouldn't be able to tell me. Some of the information sent chills down my spine.

The report talked about Nicky McNamara and his cronies and their potential connection to Damien's disappearance.

149

The extensive investigation Williams had been managing back in 2005 had seemingly drawn no conclusions. Kilbride didn't seem to think much more could be done with regards to that line of enquiry, barring the discovery of new evidence.

But that still meant that McNamara's involvement couldn't be discounted. Nor could the possibility that Damien had been murdered after being subjected to a sexual assault. Once again, the paedophile who had murdered George Mortimer, Darren Collings, was mentioned and the line of enquiry was advised to be re-examined.

Kilbride explained how he had made nine major recommendations to Hampshire Police that they would be obliged to act on. Some were straightforward, such as advising the force to action further enquiries around the people who saw or spoke to Damien between 10pm on the Saturday night and 12:30am on the Sunday morning, even going back to witnesses and taking additional statements if necessary.

Kilbride didn't try to hide his disgust at the lackadaisical approach to documentation and the taking of factual reports throughout the case. Other recommendations were specific and asked officers to address issues with the evidenced sequence of events, timings and conflicting statements. Some referred to witness statements that we'd never even been informed of. The report pressed on the police to identify the remaining three men captured on the CCTV in Yorkies as a priority.

We'd argued that point for years.

It also recommended that a number of rumours surrounding Damien's disappearance be reinvestigated, including one that a male resembling Nicky McNamara had held a youth up against a wall near the Harbour Lights pub and given the lad a beating.

Could that have been Damien?

Crucially, the report advised Hampshire Police to examine all of the new points raised between the established standard for a missing person inquiry and the MIRSAP standard – the Major Incident Room Standard Administration Procedures. The MIRSAP standard was the benchmark utilised in murder cases. It had been set in the 1970s following the Yorkshire Ripper inquiry. In the main, Ed and I were pleased with the report; the only disappointment came in the final classification of the case.

Despite all of the information – which clearly pointed more towards the potential for foul play than an accident or voluntary disappearance – Damien's case was to remain a missing person case. DCI Kilbride had concluded that there was no substantive evidence to support the theory that Damien disappeared as a direct result of murder. But he also stated that the theory could not be discounted. If that was the case, then how could the investigation *not* be a murder inquiry? It made no sense to me, but what could I say?

As we reached the end of the report, DCI Kilbride advised us that we take some time to absorb all the details and call or email him with any questions we had and he would respond. An open channel of communication! For the first time ever, I felt like someone from within the police was sympathetic to the way we had been treated and how the whole case had been managed. Someone agreed that a lack of attention to detail had caused us almost eleven years of pain. The report all but confirmed this.

I couldn't help but wonder: if Damien had been alive out there somewhere on that Sunday, might he have been helped if the police had done their job properly? This thought was further cemented when Kilbride turned to Ed and me, just before he left, and spoke solemnly.

'The loss of the CCTV from the town was extremely regrettable,' he said. 'That footage would have been a gift to any investigation.' He made his feelings clear. It was sloppy policing at its worst. Exactly what we had always thought. Coming from a man of his respected stature with Hampshire Constabulary, I'd never felt more vindicated. We couldn't bring that footage back, but at least this report meant that Hampshire Constabulary would have to go back and review Damien's case again, this time with the internal review hanging over their heads. They couldn't brush us under the carpet anymore.

* * *

Not long after delivering his verdict on the investigation to us, Kilbride retired. It came as something of a blow, as it meant we were once again left with nowhere to address our questions about the report as they arose.

Despite the initial hope the report had presented us with, the response didn't feel immediate. In fact, it took a whole month before the new team was appointed. The investigation was handed over to DI Darren O'Callaghan and, in response to guidance in DCI Kilbride's report, we were also provided with a Family Liaison Officer for the first time. His name was DI Colin Piper.

When he'd come to visit us, Kilbride had also advised that they planned to use the eleventh anniversary of Damien's disappearance to launch a new appeal. That, at least, came to fruition. We worked with the UK Police National Missing Persons Bureau (PNMPB), Parents and Abducted Children

Together (PACT) and Electronic Health Media (EHM) to appeal for new information about the case and share a photo of Damien at the time of his disappearance and an age-enhanced photo of what he might look like now, at twenty-seven years of age.

The images were shown on Missing Kids TV and also beamed across EHM's network of 129 screens in GP surgeries across England and major hospitals. It was hard to imagine Damien at twenty-seven. By that age I'd lived all over the world. I was a wife and mother. I was even pregnant with him. What might he have achieved by now? It was the second time I'd seen an age-enhanced image of Damien, but looking at this one tore at every sinew of my heart. The face staring back at me was older – he had a little less hair and a few lines around the eyes – but he was undeniably, unmistakably Damien.

My little boy.

The cheeky smile that reflected his fun personality; the joker and the tease that we all missed having around the house. Those wide eyes filled with love for his family and hope for his future. The eyes of a music lover and hard-working student, looking forward to an exciting and important career as a marine biologist.

What discoveries might he have made? Like any child, he had the potential to change the world by the very virtue of his existence. To change the lives of the people he met, as he had already touched the lives of the many people who had such positive memories of him. Would he have achieved his career goals or done something completely different? Would he still be with Gemma from Suffolk, a childhood sweetheart, or would he have met and fallen in love with someone new? Would he be married? A parent? Would he be happily single, travelling the world?

I'd never let go of the tiny sliver of hope that he was still out there somewhere. People were still discovered after years of being missing. Sometimes the circumstances were horrifying, such as being held hostage and harmed. I tried not to think about that possibility for fear it would drag me under with grief. But sometimes people were found after sustaining an injury. They'd simply forgotten who they were and started again. Or run away, only to return years later. The chances were slim, but until I knew for sure otherwise, I refused to let go of that hope.

As promised, DI O'Callaghan made a fresh appeal for information about the men from the CCTV in Yorkies, who still remained unidentified.

'Although the CCTV footage has been widely circulated in previous years, we still have not been able to identify all those who were in Yorkies fish and chip shop at the same time as Damien,' he said, as he addressed the media. 'We are using this anniversary to continue to appeal for information and we will actively pursue any lines of enquiry that arise from this publicity.'

As we waited for news, we maintained our own connections to the island, so we could source even more information about Damien's disappearance. As well as via email and through the website, we were starting to receive more and more communication through my Facebook page. Using the concept of keeping the enemy close, I accepted new friend requests almost daily. I knew that I would be provided with background from the community on the island that way.

One day it might just be of use.

I was contacted by all sorts – from journalists and councillors to current and former drug addicts. Then, one day, another individual reached out to me. He was a whole other breed. His name was Ivor Edwards. He introduced himself to me as a private investigator, published author and criminologist. He'd been following Damien's case and wanted to offer his help and expertise.

'I am sure your skills would be beneficial,' I said. 'But we couldn't afford your services.'

'Oh, I won't charge you for my services, Mrs Nettles,' he'd said with his strong London twang. 'I'll be working on a pro bono basis.'

'Why?' I asked.

'I want to help you find Damien,' he said.

I couldn't see how it would do any harm. The police had gone very quiet and nothing seemed to be moving on the case. Perhaps Ivor had some tactics up his sleeve that could unearth some new evidence?

Ivor explained that he was living on the island, in Sandown Bay. He'd stumbled on Damien's case while looking into another trial – the murder of Edwin Wilcox. I knew the name instantly from when remains had washed up at Calshot back in 1998, and when the *Isle of Wight County Press* had covered the story. The police had expected the bones to belong to either Damien or Wilcox. Once it had been confirmed that the remains belonged to neither of them, I'd more or less forgotten about Wilcox. But Ivor explained how the details surrounding the case had never rung true to him.

A man by the name of Christopher Thomas had apparently admitted to his social worker that he'd kicked Wilcox off the

200ft Culver Cliff. Wilcox had allegedly sexually abused Thomas when he'd been in a care home. The case came to court and, in the end, Thomas conducted his own defence, saying the social worker had lied. But when Wilcox's scarf was found halfway down the cliff with traces of his hair attached, investigators had a motive and evidence. Thomas was found guilty of attempted murder. As a body was never found, it was assumed that drowning and not the fall had killed Wilcox.

It was mixing with the island's murky underworld where Ivor had become aware of Damien's case. Being honest, I found him a little alarming at first. He was a crusty old bugger who pulled no punches and had no fear of the criminal fraternity *or* the law. But he was open and honest from the start. He didn't hide the fact that he had a colourful past and knew the police system intimately – from both sides.

With his background and his rich cockney accent, I honestly felt he'd be right at home with the Kray twins. But I trusted him a hell of a lot more than I did the police. You see, Ivor was a bulldog. If he got something between his teeth – a morsel of information or a bite that could be a lead – he gripped hard and wouldn't let go. Not until he had what he wanted out of it. He spoke frankly to me about witnesses and suspects. He told me he was a firm believer in Occam's razor theory, that the simplest explanation was often the answer. That was the answer he was set on getting for us.

'Suspects are like a brick wall, Valerie,' he told me. 'We are slowly chipping away at the mortar between the brick. Eventually they will crumble.'

I was sold. I liked his way of thinking and I wanted him on Damien's team.

CHAPTER FOURTEEN

AT TIMES I QUESTIONED IVOR'S METHODOLOGY. I ACCEPTED HIS approach might be a little unorthodox, but I did ask him to refrain from doing anything I wouldn't approve of. Just because we had to wade into the murky world of the criminal fraternity, didn't mean we needed to sink into the mire with them. Ivor's first action on Damien's case was to try to raise a reward fund.

'Reward money is essential after such a long passage of time,' he told me. 'It will encourage people to come forward with new information.' Neither Ivor nor our family had enough money to create an enticing reward pot, so he appealed on our behalf to large businesses on the island, like Wightlink, Tesco and Red Funnel, to provide financial support. The *Isle of Wight County Press* even published a story about it. As ever, Ivor didn't hold back. He made it clear he was critical of the police investigation.

'From the people I have already spoken to there are so many unanswered questions. The biggest unanswered question is

"Where is Damien?"' he said to the reporter. 'Police seem to have assumed he is dead but, to find out just what happened, evidence is needed. To encourage that, I think a hundred thousand pounds would be needed, and I would welcome all offers from companies and individuals. I am sure we can get to the truth.'

The idea was that the reward would only be paid if it led to a result, a solid piece of evidence that could lead to a conviction or similar. That way we wouldn't end up wasting time on wild goose chases.

His appeal did get the attention of the intended businesses, but we soon found out that a Tesco representative had approached the Isle of Wight police to take advice, should they wish to offer support. The police response had apparently been cut and dried. The representative said that the island police had advised the supermarket not to put up any money regarding a reward.

One by one, interested companies went silent. Ivor was being stonewalled. Not long after he got involved, he confided in me about a meeting he'd had with an officer on Damien's case prior to making contact with me. He'd been in touch with the police to say he was looking into the case from a professional perspective as a writer and private investigator. After arranging a meeting, a lone, plain-clothes detective had turned up at Ivor's home. He wasn't happy about Ivor's interest in the case.

'We advise you to leave this case alone. We know what happened to Damien, so you're wasting your time,' the detective had said.

'So what did happen to Damien?' Ivor had asked.

'Damien was on drugs and swam from the Isle of Wight across

the Solent around midnight to see his sister who was at college in Portsmouth,' he told Ivor. 'Damien drowned and the tides and currents would have taken him to the Hook of Holland.'

Ivor had been left offended and speechless.

'I was insulted that anyone would expect me to believe such a cock and bull story,' he'd told me, incandescent with rage. 'No Olympic swimmer on this planet would have swum across the Solent in the conditions that night, let alone a sixteen-year-old lad.'

I was livid too. The drowning theory was long discounted. And it had never been proven that Damien had taken drugs, only that he'd drunk cider. It might not be impossible. But what gave them the right to throw speculation around so carelessly? How dare they be so flippant and insensitive? I'd long gone past worrying about upsetting the police, so I lodged another complaint. This time regarding the detective Ivor had spoken to and his 'cock and bull' story. Ivor wasn't bothered about ruffling their feathers. The police had made it clear they did not wish Ivor to continue his enquiries under any circumstances. But telling Ivor not to do something was a very bad idea. It only made him more determined.

He promptly continued with his investigations on our behalf. His approach worked.

A few weeks after the article about the reward appeal had appeared, the newspaper received an anonymous letter. The author had asked that it be passed on to Ivor. It read:

Dear Ivor Edwards
It may be a rumour but I believe it's more, as I've been told by many people. Damien was down Cowes town,

drunk, shouting out things like, 'I want some fucking drugs, sell me some drugs, give me some drugs,' or words to that effect. He was doing this outside a known drug dealer's flat. The flat was above the old butcher's shop, opposite the arcade over the junction from the Pier View pub, on the middle floor. I'd been to the flat before to buy weed. There were usually faces of the criminal world inside. People a lot older. Apparently what happened was that Damien ended up inside the flat, either let in or dragged in, once in he either got punched or was hit over the head with something. I don't know how many times or by how many people, but he ended up on the floor unconscious or dead. The one name that I heard had done part of the hitting was Nicky. The main suspect who is now dead. Then the body was wrapped in chicken wire somewhere, put in the boot of a car and the body dropped off the back of the island somewhere over a cliff. I've been told the police have investigated this.

Anonymous 2327

I honestly didn't know how to feel when Ivor brought the letter to me. It corroborated a number of rumours that we'd heard year after year. The claim that Damien had been seen shouting up to a flat in town, that there had been an argument over drugs, that he'd been killed and disposed of. But without a sworn statement everything remained speculation – information the police refused to countenance.

'If only these people would openly come forward with

statements like these,' I said to Ivor. 'Maybe then we could establish the veracity of these rumours.'

But we both agreed that some things in the letter didn't ring true. No other accounts had suggested Damien was being aggressive or swearing. The video footage we had seen showed his mood had been completely the opposite. What were we meant to believe? The one key factor for me was that name turning up again, like a bad penny: Nicky McNamara. In every account he was there. The passage of time had allowed Damien's story to morph into an island mystery. A tale filled with bad guys and bogeymen. By appealing for information and asking people to come to us directly, we'd made Damien's story public property.

People did come forward. We heard about noise near Bars Hill that had sounded like a fight, and a vague account of a youth being held up against a wall in that area at a similar time. But so much was of little use. There was no hard evidence. Sometimes I wondered if people said things just to be a part of it. It was a strange morbid quirk I had noticed over time.

Damien's disappearance was an urban myth now. Fact had melded with fiction. But among all the exaggerations and embellishments there *had* to be some truth. A constant that would reveal the thread of what really happened. And Nicky McNamara was always there. What was his connection to Damien? Ivor pressed to find out more, while also investigating other lines of enquiry. Before long, he'd found out more about the circumstances of McNamara's death.

I was told that he was a heroin addict. He'd last been seen by his landlady, a woman named Shirley Barrett, on the morning of Saturday 21 September 2002 in a house on Prospect Road, in Newport. He'd gone to the bathroom to take some heroin. She'd taken the drug too. It was clear the house was no ordinary home. *It was a drug house.*

Ivor even discovered that the main suspect in the Edwin Wilcox murder case, Christopher Thomas, lived in the same house on Prospect Road with his partner at the time Damien disappeared. They were married and she was called Shirley Thomas. It didn't take Ivor long to work out that Shirley Thomas and Shirley Barrett were one and the same. When I saw pictures of Shirley, she looked vaguely familiar. Then I remembered her. At least, a much younger version.

'She used to strut down Cowes High Street with her mangy dog and a tattooed bloke with a Mohican,' I said to Ivor. 'I'd cross the road to avoid her.'

'You'd be right to,' Ivor said.

Turns out she was infamous on the drug scene. The house that Nicky had died in had even been nicknamed 'the House of Death' on account of all the people who'd overdosed there over the years. The details of McNamara's death were gruesome. At an inquest in 2003, the coroner ruled that he'd died of a drug overdose from heroin injected into his back. His body hadn't been found for almost three days, despite other people being in the house. He was found naked and curled up in an empty bath with two syringes on the floor beside him, along with some clothes and a towel. A doctor said that he could have died up to forty-eight hours before he was discovered. His family believed the death was suspicious. At the time, Shirley hadn't turned up to the inquest. Apparently she'd had a migraine.

'I think I'd have had a headache if I was her too,' quipped

Ivor. 'It was all quite suspicious.' He was right. Why hadn't Nicky been found sooner? Had no one needed to use the toilet all weekend? Why was there no water in the bath? How would someone inject themselves in their own back?

Two statements from Shirley were read out in court. She said that she and McNamara had injected heroin on the Friday night along with a second man, Sean Michael Thompson. She said she'd woken up on the sofa the following morning, gone upstairs and seen McNamara sitting up in the bath, having a 'dig'. I learned this was a term meaning to inject heroin.

They'd exchanged a few words but she hadn't bothered him after that, as she said he could get violent. It seems the drug binge had continued all weekend, as she claimed the other man, Thompson, woke her up on Monday morning with a cup of tea. After that, Thompson had discovered McNamara's body in the bath.

Despite the questions raised by McNamara's family, based on the findings of the pathologist, the coroner recorded a verdict of self-induced drug overdose. A newspaper article found by Ivor also explained that the other man from the house, Thompson, was also now dead. He'd taken his own life. He was found hanged on the New Year's Eve following McNamara's death. It was a grubby story that made my skin crawl. Looking at the information we had at face value, there was at least one attempted murder, a suspicious drug death and a suicide. Was any of it connected to Damien's disappearance?

Ivor's progress and our commitment to keeping Damien's name in the public eye was in stark contrast to that of the police. In time another local resolution was agreed, this time regarding my complaint about the detective's comments to Ivor about Damien – a simple slap on the wrist. I wasn't really surprised. Nor was Ivor. Once again, we just carried on, undeterred. While he continued seeking answers from people on the island, I'd been working with Nicki Durbin, the mother of Luke Durbin, a missing boy from Ipswich, and her friend Jill Blonsky, to arrange a 'March for the Missing'. Corran had made contact with Nicki after seeing her talk about her son Luke being missing and asked if she could introduce her to me via email. She'd told Nicki about Damien's story and said that hearing her speak had been just like listening to me. We were experiencing the same feelings. Nicki agreed immediately and we'd been in touch ever since.

In the years since Damien had disappeared, I'd become part of a community of people with missing loved ones – people like Nicki – and over that time I had come to realise the extent of the issue. More than 200,000 people are reported missing each year, yet there is little support from official bodies. The National Missing Persons Helpline is the only real source of guidance for us and for other families affected by the issue. We became acutely aware that their government funding had been reduced. They really didn't have the money to sustain the needs of the magnitude of the issue. As much as I wanted to find Damien, I wanted to use our family's pain to make a positive change too. To make a difference.

Nicki felt the same. We wanted to highlight the missing persons issue and raise awareness of the plight of those left behind: parents, siblings, friends and partners. The idea really grew out of our frustration with the lack of government funding for the charity and how missing person cases and the families of missing people were often dealt with in an unequal manner.

Nicki's son Luke had gone missing twelve months before
Madeleine McCann, and in the same year that the 'Suffolk
Strangler' had murdered five women in Ipswich. Between
Maddie and the serial murder case, she'd struggled to get much
media coverage for Luke. His story seemed to get overlooked. A
missing teenage boy just couldn't compete with an angelic lost
little girl and a string of grisly murders. I knew that as well as
Nicki did. We didn't resent the coverage Maddie's case received
– in fact we were delighted for the McCanns – but it was the
kind of profile we could only dream of for our boys.

In our minds, *every* missing person – especially a child –
should be afforded the same opportunities. We knew media
airtime would always be limited, so we felt some procedures
and standards should be put in place to support the families of
all missing people.

We needed to be seen and understood. What's more, many
families like us needed practical and financial support too. So
we decided to do something about it. We didn't really have a
clue how to proceed. We just muddled through. We had ideas
and we made them happen.

Jill had organised a march before, so we drew on that
expertise, while Nicki worked hard to coordinate the event
with the Metropolitan Police. A man called Matt Searle, from a
charity called Missing Abroad, created some posters for us and
together we wrote content for our promotional material. On a
wing and a prayer we set up a Facebook group and asked other
families in our position to join us on the march. We invited
them to come together to be a voice in unison, speaking to the
authorities, the government and the people of the UK. Along
with the details of where and when the march would take place,

together we wrote a piece explaining what the event was about and posted it in the group.

We wanted government support; better training for police, and even a dedicated branch of the force for missing person cases. We wanted the missing issue to be addressed as a national crisis and funds to support, counsel and advise to be made available. We wanted to give families like our own a voice. *The families of the forgotten missing.*

After months of planning I flew back to London to represent Damien at the march.

The group had a positive response, but we still had no idea if anyone would actually turn up.

My stomach was in knots as we gathered at the Raoul Wallenberg statue in Great Cumberland Place, but one by one they loosened as faces began to appear. In the end, around 100 people marched with Nicki and I through London, including Sarah's friend, Scott Bradley, members of our family including my brother Nigel, sister Sally, brother-in-law Clive, a friend from back home in America called Lynn Kimmel and my good friend Fiona Prentice. We travelled from Great Cumberland Place to Trafalgar Square with a full police escort, stopping traffic as we moved through the city.

I was filled with emotion as we held a ceremony at our destination, reading out the names of just some missing people, including Damien's. We listed the goals in a manifesto, which we would later present to our local MPs. The missing issue wasn't new, and it wasn't one that would go away anytime soon, so those affected by it needed structured, official support – emotional, financial and practical. It was an exhausting and exhilarating day, worth every bit of effort.

After the march, which was attended by representatives from the National Missing Persons Helpline – which had recently been rebranded as the Missing People charity – we met with the CEO of the organisation, Paul Tuohy. He fully agreed with, and was committed to the principles we'd laid out and agreed to take the suggestions forward on behalf of our families and the missing. It felt like our message was heard. The ball was finally rolling for getting formal help and guidelines in place to support the families left behind, not to mention future families who would be affected.

Focusing on the bigger issues surrounding missing people gave me a sense of purpose and kept Damien in the media spotlight as well. In any coverage of the march I was referred to as 'Valerie Nettles, mother of Damien Nettles, who has been missing since 1996'.

Organising the march had been profoundly important to me. You see, as we waited for the recommendations from the Kilbride report to be actioned, I began to question who I was.

It was a question that had bubbled under the surface for years. Probably since the moment we realised that Damien had vanished.

Living in the USA I'd fallen into a routine – a strange cycle of being without really living. I woke up each day at around 5:15am, made coffee then checked my emails. My emails were my lifeline to the island and to Damien's case. They were my first thought each morning. They were also my connection to the families of other missing people, like Nicki Durbin, to whom I had grown close. I'd leaned on them in times of need and offered a supportive shoulder when they needed it too.

After catching up on emails I would shower, brush my teeth,

dry my hair, put on my make-up and get dressed. Every day I would throw myself together like this. Make myself passable in appearance. But every day, as I caught a glimpse of myself in the mirror, I'd be struck by the same thought.

Why? I would ask my reflection. *Why are you still functioning? Your son is out there somewhere. He's probably in a shallow grave and here you are getting ready for work. Why?*

Having no answer, I'd look away and just carry on. Breathing, functioning, but not living. I worked hard but my heart simply wasn't in my job. It was always back on the Isle of Wight, back where Damien disappeared. I lived constantly with one foot back in 1996 and the other foot firmly in the present – buried under the thoughts, fears and precious memories. It was impossible for me to go back, but I would never be able to move forward without some form of resolution. It had taken me almost a decade to realise: *that was who I was – the mother of a missing child. One who had possibly been murdered.*

Everything else around me – my work and any social activities I chose to participate in – held no substance. My daily routine was a gossamer veil, faintly hiding the pain and anguish that lay beneath. That was how I lived with my reality. In a way, accepting that feeling gave me strength. As the mother of a missing child I had a responsibility to Damien, to find out what had happened to him. But I also felt a responsibility to the families of other missing people – present and future. This meant sharing my experiences and demanding that changes be made, so that the pain of a loved one disappearing could be eased even slightly for those after us.

It meant not being scared to take on the authorities and demanding fair treatment.

So when, in September 2008, I discovered that both DI O'Callaghan and DI Piper had been seconded on to other investigations, I was more than ready to go into battle with our local police force once again. We'd had no communication for three months and it wasn't good enough.

I wasn't going to let Damien get pushed down their priorities again.

CHAPTER FIFTEEN

I MADE MY DISAPPOINTMENT ABOUT THE SILENCE AND INACTION from the not-so 'dedicated' team on Damien's case perfectly clear in yet another complaint to Hampshire Constabulary. I was also sure to remind them of the findings of the Kilbride review. It didn't even bother me to complain now. In the early days I'd been nervous and worried. Nowadays, it just felt like part of the process. Police go quiet, I get proactive. Police miraculously appear to be taking action. On the surface, at least.

True to form, around six weeks after I'd questioned why I hadn't heard from DI O'Callaghan, a fresh appeal for information came out of Hampshire Constabulary. When the story hit the local paper, I had to laugh at the headline: POLICE BRING NEW HOPE TO DAMIEN HUNT. If only people knew how hard we'd had to push for this 'new hope'.

The appeal was hardly groundbreaking, but it did appear to be angled towards some of the recommendations in Kilbride's report. It explained how all the detail of Damien's case had been uploaded into a new section on Hampshire Constabulary's website, called Casebook.

It was a place where information about ongoing investigations was kept. Damien's page contained the age-enhanced image of him and the video footage from Yorkies. Alongside it was a plea for information that might identify those men in the chip shop that night, who still, twelve years on, hadn't been found.

O'Callaghan was quoted in the article in the *Isle of Wight County Press*. He said: 'I'm asking everyone who was in Cowes on November 2nd, 1996, to dig deep into their memories for any small piece of information or detail that might provide a vital clue to Damien's movements on the night he was last seen. People have come forward years after Damien's disappearance was first publicised, which suggests there is still the possibility members of the community may know something that could take the investigation forward.'

I always tried to remain hopeful, but I wasn't foolish enough to believe that Damien's case was suddenly a priority. I'd been stung too many times for that. While we waited for information to come in, we put our own measures into place: other ways to keep Damien's name alive and information coming in. I requested the CCTV to upload to Damien's website to support the appeal, as I had sent our VCR copy to a magazine as part of an interview I'd done about Damien's case. Eventually I was provided with a CD copy, made after it had been sent away for enhancement. Ed and I watched it through to make sure it worked properly but, as we did, we noticed something unusual.

'Didn't a police car drive past at one point?' I remembered.

'You're right,' he replied. We fast-forwarded and rewound

trying to find it, then we noticed something – the time on the clock skipped forward. *The tape had been spliced.*

'Why would they do that?' I asked. I contacted DI O'Callaghan for an explanation.

'This is done for sound operational reasons,' he said. 'We cut segments out so witnesses could confirm what has happened in the missing bits. To test their veracity.' It made sense, but the fact that it edited out the police car made me uneasy. Was it just a coincidence? Or were they trying to hide something?

Time marched ever forward yet we stayed suspended in limbo. There were special days and big life events, of course. In recent years Damien had become an uncle several times over. James and his wife Melissa had even given their first boy, Robert, the middle name Damien in tribute to the uncle he'd never met. As a family we did our best to make sure he was remembered. When O'Callaghan arranged for Damien to be included in an International Missing Children's Day event at the South Bank in London, in May 2009, my brother Nigel attended on our behalf, joining other relatives of missing people, including Kate and Gerry McCann.

It highlighted eighty-five missing children, including Damien. But the heartbreaking fact was that number didn't even scratch the surface. There were tens of thousands more out there. I wondered how many of their families had suffered as we had? Had to fight for police to keep searching. To keep the media interested? Probably all of them, as time had gone on.

I knew now better than anyone that a fresh missing person story would capture hearts and minds. An old one with no news and no resolution became a burden. At least that's what it felt like with the police. My life had become one fraught with despair and anxiety. Most nights I lay awake in bed with questions swirling through my mind.

When will it stop?

When can we have a normal life?

When can I stop fighting?

When can I bury my son?

It was like relentless screaming, over and over and over. But I knew the answer. For me, Ed, Sarah, James and Melissa, it wouldn't stop. Not until we found Damien, dead or alive.

* * *

At the turn of the new decade, everything around us was changing. In fact the only thing that seemed to stand still was progress on Damien's case. Getting information out of the police was like wading through treacle. We were met with resistance and a defensive tone every time we dared ask for an update.

At one point we'd had a huge boost, when DI O'Callaghan had informed us of more developments in DNA testing. He'd said that new technology meant they might be able to take DNA from Damien's beloved guitar strings, which we still had with us in America. It could then be used to try and link up some of the other strands of information the police had. But to collect the DNA he would need to come to us. It was an option that was blocked by Hampshire Constabulary, due to lack of resources. O'Callaghan had tried to be innovative, looking for another way to move things forward. We appreciated his efforts, but we knew he could only do so much. If the top brass didn't support the idea, where else could he go?

Once again, the big blue wall shut down a glimmer of hope. Eventually, O'Callaghan faded off the case. He was still our SIO but, in October 2010, a gentleman called DI Nick Heelan began working in tandem with him. I never received another Family Liaison Officer, but Heelan was quite the breath of fresh air. He was a nice, friendly and helpful policeman and was more communicative than his predecessors.

Not long after Heelan came on board, James received a worrying text message. It was from a man claiming to be one of Nicky McNamara's associates. In the message he told James he had information about where Damien was, but that no one would listen to him. We could only assume by 'no one' he meant the police. He said Damien was buried on a cycle track. We pondered over the message. The only place we could think of was an old railway line between Cowes and Newport that was sometimes called the 'cycle track', locally. We passed the information over to DI O'Callaghan and DI Heelan. While they promised to look into it, O'Callaghan made it clear he didn't think much of the source. They'd spoken before and he thought he couldn't be trusted.

Heelan pushed hard, though. Like us, he knew there were people on the island that were now willing to talk. Whether it was guilt, or because they were no longer afraid to speak out, it was happening. He even told us that he hoped the case would be upgraded to a suspected murder case. But another month passed without any news or update. It honestly felt like we were never going to get anywhere, no matter what information we passed to the police. Until one day Heelan emailed with some news.

'I've got a meeting with my superior, Mr Harris,' he said. 'He wants me to clarify some points before we escalate the case.' I punched the air with joy. It was finally happening. I called Ed immediately.

'Are you sitting down?' I said, excitedly. I knew the news would blow him away too.

'What is it?' he asked.

'They're going to escalate the case.'

'Finally,' said Ed. 'They're actually doing what they should have done at the start of all this.'

To say we were over the moon was an understatement. At last, after so many years of pushing, we were finally getting to grips with the truth. The police were finally showing an appreciation of the seriousness of Damien's case.

While we waited to hear back from DI Heelan and the team, we focused on raising awareness of Damien's investigation and the wider missing people issue too. To commemorate the fourteenth anniversary of Damien's disappearance in November 2010 we pulled together – our family, Damien's friends and businesses from the island that supported us, such as Wight Local, Wight Quote, Vectis Radio and *Isle of Wight Gazette*. We raised enough money to hire a billboard in Newport town centre.

Our good friend Carmelle James, who was the driving force behind the idea, approached the billboard company and arranged for us to hire it for ten whole days. The poster was even provided free of charge by a local printing firm called Biltmore Printers. The twenty-metre by ten-metre billboard would display a huge picture of Damien, the date of his disappearance, his description and the numbers for the police, Missing People and Crimestoppers. As well as that, the YMCA in Newport were printing T-shirts with Damien's picture and the Missing People website address on for us. Local high school and college kids pledged to wear them, like human billboards. Damien would be everywhere, staring from every angle. Forcing people to remember. Making them think about the things they might have seen that night in 1996. *The things they might have been doing at that time.*

I wondered if the sight of his sweet, innocent face might gnaw at the conscience of anyone who was there, or who knew something. Maybe it would prompt those people who were thinking about speaking out to take action. Although I knew there were still so many possibilities, my mind focused on the constant in so many stories: Nicky McNamara. He might be dead, but what about his friends and family? His associates?

Ivor heard of one man, allegedly an associate of Nicky's, who couldn't help but talk about Damien when he was drunk. Repeating over and again the same thing: 'No body, no crime.'

Maybe some remained loyal, but others didn't. We knew at least one that was already willing to speak. Would more of them finally crumble? Had we chipped away enough at the mortar between the brick of the island's criminal fraternity?

CHAPTER SIXTEEN

A MONTH ON FROM THE BILLBOARD CAMPAIGN WE RECEIVED AN update from the police. I'd hoped it might be some new intelligence shared by someone who had seen the poster. But it wasn't. It was about DI Heelan. He emailed us to let us know that he would be moving on from the Major Crimes team due to personal reasons. He assured us a new SIO would be appointed in due course. Damien's case was like a revolving door. Constantly changing faces. Who would the next person be? Would they give my son's case the care it deserved? We didn't have to wait long to find out.

In January 2011, DCI David Powell introduced himself as our new SIO and DI Heelan's supervisor. When we first spoke over the phone, he seemed genuine in wanting to get results. The communication continued on a fortnightly basis, when he would ring us with updates, no matter how small. By mid-March his operation had even delivered an update on something we'd been chasing for years – the identity of the other men in the chip shop that night with Damien.

On Powell's instruction they had gone back to the army HQ in Aldershot and shared images of the men. In a matter of days they had all been identified as serving soldiers who had been out in Cowes. There was no feedback about what they knew – I didn't even know if they had been interviewed – but at least we now knew who they were. Why had it taken fifteen years to give us that?

While he seemed quite effective, we noticed that DCI Powell's email contact was minimal. He said he preferred phone calls, as tone could easily be misread in emails, but it left me with a disjointed paper trail. I wondered if it was also a choice in response to the history of this case and that I was able to clearly articulate my concerns. It was hard to tell. We still didn't have a new FLO, but that was par for the course.

According to DCI Powell, he was my FLO as well as the SIO. He said it would cut out the 'middleman', but I knew it wouldn't work like that. SIOs were far too busy to respond to the kinds of questions I would want to direct to a FLO. All we could do was hope that Powell's improved communication would be matched by the action he took on the case.

But despite his desire to get results, Powell made it clear he would only act on solid fact. Acting as FLO and SIO he was able to dismiss most of the existing theories as gossip, third-hand information or lies. Every person who came forward, or whom we suggested as a possible witness, he usually deemed unreliable because they were drug addicts and were unable to recall events clearly or were mentally unfit. He told me people often admitted to crimes they could not have committed. Still, it never ceased to baffle me.

If there were some reason to believe that drugs were an

issue in any police case, witnesses would be likely from that world. But did that always make their testimonies unreliable? Surely some of the information was worth investigating. I sometimes doubted if the police cared to solve this case at all. Their dismissive approach at times plunged me into a pit of despair.

I think DCI Powell had expected me to back down or quietly accept his opinion. He soon found that I was not going to give in that easily. I'd been fighting for more than fourteen years. I hoped he didn't think I was going to stop now. As my frustration with the police continued, albeit slightly diluted thanks to Powell's regular and friendly calls, our own investigations had a positive result.

A source had come forward to a friend of ours. From what she told us, we believed it to be the same man that had texted James a few months earlier. He'd asked to make contact with us again. He liked and trusted James, it seemed, so he texted him what was on his mind.

He said that eight years previously he'd told the police what had happened to Damien – that Nicky McNamara had killed him.

This time, though, he went into much greater detail. He said there had been an argument over some cannabis. Nicky had thrown a punch at Damien in anger, but hadn't intended to kill him. He then explained intricately where Damien's body had been hidden, in a renowned drugs den in Cowes. On Fellows Road.

The name rang a bell. I knew it was the same street that the Boons had lived on. Suddenly I recalled the chat Conny and I had many years earlier – about people saying they saw kids coming and going from the house at the end of her road. Everything fell into place.

The informant told me he had been kept there for up to two weeks before being buried near a cycle path in a sail bag. The detail he provided made me sick to my stomach. To think that my boy might have been treated in such a way; that he'd been so close to people who were desperately looking for him.

It was such a detailed account from someone very close to those people that we felt there might be some truth there somewhere. His information was specific and consistent. Despite his connections he seemed remarkably honest. His story had never changed. I couldn't understand why it didn't warrant a look. It seemed more than just gossip. I reported everything directly to DCI Powell and reminded him about the information we had passed to Heelan and O'Callaghan a few months earlier. I told him every single tiny detail he had shared.

By now, I'd learned our informant was married into the drugs world and I wasn't sure how highly Powell would rate this information. But I also hoped he could not ignore the level of detail. And the fact local police had allegedly dismissed the information twice. If the information turned out to be good and they ignored it, they would risk looking inept. I knew that was something Powell wouldn't stand for, but I think he could also see the same glimmer of hope that we did.

That we might be getting somewhere. At last.

Not long after I passed over the information, my gut feeling was confirmed. Powell contacted me. He wanted to let me know that, based on new and existing intelligence, a search was about to be mounted. Police would be looking at the places the informant had mentioned and the people he had named. He told me it would take a few months to plan but was sure that, if executed properly, the operation would lead to arrests.

'So many people have put themselves in the picture,' he said to me. 'Let them put their money where their mouths are.'

His plan was to arrest those who either claimed knowledge or were named as being involved in Damien's alleged killing, to see if they would crack or grass on one another. Much like Ivor's approach, chipping away at whatever it was that bound them together. It was the most definitive action I'd known the police to take in over fourteen years. Powell seemed cautiously optimistic that it would deliver some kind of result. I had to put my faith in him.

And let Hampshire Police put its money where its mouth was too.

We left the force to prepare its operation. In the meantime Sarah and I made a planned visit back to the island to attend a gig some friends had organised at The Anchor in Cowes. The aim was to remember Damien while also raising money for organisations supporting the families of missing people. It was our way of continuing to try and make a difference. Turning our pain into something positive.

The bands and artists at the gig were a mix of local acts like Gareth Icke and EnglanE, and Damien's own childhood friends. Chris Boon was now the lead singer in a band called Pleasurade, who performed alongside Damien's old bandmate Alex Roberts, who was now a solo artist. The pub was packed to the rafters, filled with familiar faces, laughing, singing, dancing and catching up. It was a wonderful evening, exactly the kind of event that Damien would have loved. Looking around the room, I imagined what it would be like to see him standing at the bar and sipping a pint with his mates. Bobbing his head to the beat of the music or, more importantly, he'd be performing – up there with his friends jamming on his guitar.

A wave of emotion washed over me. That wasn't our reality. Damien wasn't here and we still didn't know why. After fourteen years there were still no answers. No cross, no marker, no place we could go and visit to pay our respects. Nothing. There were no words for what I felt. It was an ache and an emptiness – a void that couldn't be filled. Sarah must have recognised the look in my eyes, as she came over and wrapped her arms around me.

'Damien would have loved this line-up,' she said, squeezing me tightly. Tears pricked my eyes. I knew she was feeling it too – the ache and the emptiness. She had lost her brother and best friend, after all. We all lived with it, day in and day out. But the love of our friends, family and supporters on the island buoyed us. By turning out for the gig, each and every person reminded us that, like us, they hadn't forgotten Damien. Like us, they still wanted answers. As I moved through the bar area, I suddenly spotted a familiar figure. Big and tall, his frame took up so much space in the cramped pub.

'Davey Boon,' I said, smiling as I approached him. It was Chris's little brother, whom Damien had been with at the party on the night he disappeared.

'Hi Val,' he said, smiling shyly.

We stood for a while and chatted. I asked how he was. It seemed he'd left the band he'd been in with his brother due to ongoing commitments and the stress of working and performing. He also told me he was a born-again Christian, something I recalled from when he'd been in touch a while back. He'd had a few theories of his own about Damien's disappearance that he wanted to share. Before long I moved on, leaving him to enjoy the show. It wasn't long before I bumped into his mum and dad, Conny and John.

'Did you see Davey?' Conny asked.

'I did,' I replied. 'We had a nice chat.'

'That's so nice he spoke to you,' she said, surprised.

'Of course,' I said. 'I was pleased to talk to him. Why is it a surprise?'

'He's become a bit introverted these days,' she replied. 'I'm glad you caught up.'

I was glad too. But seeing all of my kids' friends and their parents whom we'd known since they were children was bittersweet. I was acutely aware of the passage of time and how much life had been lived that Damien had not been able to enjoy. I had kept in touch over the years with many of them via social media. I would hear from them occasionally on Facebook or from one of my kids, who would update me on what was going on in everyone's lives.

Chris and Davey of course let me know when the police had them in for questioning.

It had happened on a number of occasions over the years. I understood that the police needed to interrogate thoroughly those last seen with Damien. But I was sorry for that too, for their sake. It was a tough thing for such young teenagers to have to deal with on top of losing a friend. I couldn't help but wonder how it might have affected them.

I still wrestled with my emotions, and the guilt of allowing Damien to stay out later that night. Had the situation left the

THE BOY WHO DISAPPEARED

boys with emotional scars and feelings of guilt deep down too? Things that would trouble or disturb them? I doubted there was much help available for them to talk about what had happened. I was sure that they had nothing to do with it.

I trusted Chris. I liked him as much as Damien had, which was a lot. They were so funny together and never failed to make me chuckle. Their giddy ways, combined with their love of music, meant they'd always reminded me of Bill and Ted from the film *Bill and Ted's Excellent Adventure.* Carefree, kind-hearted and as silly as they came. Seeing both Boon boys, especially Chris and his band, was really nice. Chris was married and a father now. Like his brother, and so many of Damien's friends, they were taking charge of their own lives.

Of course I wondered occasionally if there was anything they might have known as teenagers that they may have been afraid to talk about; it was only natural. Rumours were rife about local thugs and dealers who would beat up kids who even looked at them the wrong way. Whenever the thought crossed my mind, I hoped this had not been the case for them. That they hadn't been afraid or pressured. I felt sure that, by now, Damien's friends had told everything they knew, even if they'd been too scared back in the day. You only had to look around the packed pub to see how much they all cared. The fact was, without any information about where Damien was or what happened, all we could do was accept, trust and have faith in others to do the right thing. I was aware that something this traumatic happening to kids usually called for counselling. They were all so young and it surely must have left some lasting effects that were hard to shake.

I recognised pretty much everyone in the pub that night, or at least knew whom they were connected to – spouses, kids and bandmates. But there was one figure that stood out to me. He was familiar, but I was struggling to remember his name. He was a boy that Damien always spoke of as one of the naughty kids from his school. They weren't 'friends' as such, but, with the island being so small, they all inevitably hung out together in large extended groups. To my surprise, he came over. Even before he spoke, I could see he was in an agitated state. And he appeared to be as high as a kite.

'Damien treated me right when everyone else at school didn't,' he said. 'I had a lot of respect for him.'

'That's very kind of you to say,' I replied. 'Thank you.'

He looked at me for a moment. Like there was more he wanted to say, but just as he opened his mouth to speak another boy appeared. I didn't recognise him, but they were clearly friends.

'I'll have to go,' he said, shuffling away. I frowned. What more was he going to say? I didn't notice them again until the end of the night, when I spotted them with a couple of Damien's friends, huddled at the back gate of the pub's garden. I didn't think anything of it, since they had all gone to school together. But the next evening, while we were out for a drink locally, one of the boys' mothers took my brother Nigel aside.

'My son was told to "back off" last night,' she said, nervously.

'From what?' asked Nigel.

'Appeals for Damien,' she said, her voice hushed.

The threats, I was told, had come from those two lads. It was a chilling thought, but when I asked Damien's friends about it directly, they denied it or played it down. Who was I to believe? An adult, who was a professional person, or these kids that Damien had grown up with, who may still be afraid of local thugs? I couldn't see why either would lie. Unless someone was scared . . . Eventually, through asking around, I got the name of the 'naughty kid' and passed it on to Ivor.

As soon as I said his name Ivor recognised it. He'd been mentioned in one of the many stories about Damien's disappearance. It was claimed that some men in a red van abducted and murdered Damien. This kid had allegedly seen this and run off.

He was a potential witness.

I sent this information straight to Powell, who promised to look into it. I guess I shouldn't have been surprised. Our presence on the island was always noticed. Our fundraising events generated media coverage, which in turn splashed Damien across newspapers and online, raising the speculation levels again. That made some people nervous.

Some people wanted Damien to be forgotten. We never quite knew why. Maybe our visits were very uncomfortable for people with a guilty conscience.

Well, good. I wanted them to be reminded of whatever it was they'd done.

What they'd seen.

What they knew.

I also noticed that when we were back on the Isle of Wight we received more Facebook requests and messages, more emails, and sometimes we were even approached by people who wanted to speak to us in person. This visit was no different. At the end of the event at The Anchor, Sarah was approached by a young man who had helped organise it. She told me he'd seemed extremely anxious and said he needed to speak with us.

We met him at the Woodvale Hotel the next day. He brought his mother, who poured out a long and troubling story about how two of her sons had got into drugs and on the wrong side of the island's dealers. It only served to remind me of the alarming extent of the problem that had riddled the island in the 1990s at the time when Damien would have been growing up. How it had earned its reputation as a smuggler's haven.

But what did it all have to do with Damien?

'We've heard Damien upset a well-known crooked business-man,' she said. It was a long and involved story but she alluded to one of the local thugs sent to 'sort Damien out'.

'Who was it?' I asked.

'Nicky McNamara,' she replied.

CHAPTER SEVENTEEN

FOUR MONTHS AFTER HE'D TOLD US OF HIS PLANS TO UNDERTAKE a number of searches, DCI Powell made good on his word. A team was prepared and a search was focused on a key location identified by police intelligence.

We'd passed the information we'd heard at the Woodvale Hotel on to DCI Powell, but we didn't know how much it would help. The story suggested that a big-name island businessman, who was alleged to be part of a seedy network, had put a 'hit' out on Damien for apparently standing up to some of his nasty dealings.

Damien had stood up for the right thing more than once in his life. He'd always back the underdogs at school, and even once came home from a night out with a black eye after he'd challenged a man he'd seen hitting his girlfriend. But he knew his limits.

This story struck me as a bit far-fetched but it was gripping nevertheless and it scared both Sarah and me. DCI Powell's response to the information was typical. He said he believed the family had an agenda and that they were using Damien as a means to an end for their own benefit. He seemed well acquainted with the family and simply blew the story off. It wasn't so easy for us. It never was. Once again, there we were left with all sorts of terrible visions and theories spinning in our minds. Left wondering if there was a thread of truth in what we'd heard.

The only real glimmer of interest from the story was Nicky McNamara being in the picture and a potential location for Damien's body. They'd named Parkhurst Forest as a burial site, something we'd also heard from a handful of other sources. As Powell's sting swung into action, Operation Ridgewood was finally escalated from a missing person case to one where murder or foul play could not be ruled out. That was a victory in itself for us. According to Powell, the 'new' police intelligence was acquired from leads that had been followed up over the course of twelve months, many of which had come from our informant. *The one they'd dismissed in the past.*

On the morning of 10 May 2011, a dawn raid took place on a number of addresses across the island. The idea was to take the targets of the operation by surprise. That day, five people were arrested and questioned at different police stations. We weren't privy to the names of the suspects but we were given whatever detail was permitted:

- A 48-year-old man from Sandown, Isle of Wight.
- A 45-year-old man from Cowes, Isle of Wight.
- A 50-year-old man from Newport, Isle of Wight.
- A 37-year-old man from Ryde, Isle of Wight.
- A 40-year-old man from Gravesend, Kent.

I couldn't be certain, but as I cross-referenced the names that had been connected with Damien's disappearance time and again, with the scant details we had, I could hazard a good guess at the names of some of the people they'd taken in.

Powell was pleased with the outcome and I was delighted to see some action. But I did wonder if they planned to look at *all* the places identified as where Damien's body might have been dumped after he was killed. It soon emerged that officers were only combing the marshland along the Cowes to Newport cycle track, near Stag Lane. The inch-by-inch search by a team of ten divers was expected to last into the following week. But why just there? It seemed a wasted opportunity when they had all these resources and manpower available to them.

A couple of days after the dawn raids, the *Isle of Wight County Press* covered the news of the arrests. Powell called them a 'breakthrough', but to my dismay he said they were not planning on searching any further sites. A deluge of other emotions compounded my disappointment and frustration. We had suspected it for years, but the escalation of the case made it real: *Damien may have been murdered.*

It was strange how the official acknowledgement from the police overwhelmed us all. James and his family were living with me and Ed in Dallas, suspended in limbo as we waited for news, while Sarah and Melissa were in touch daily from their homes in Seattle, Washington and Lubbock, Texas. The pain and anguish was as fresh as ever.

As the search continued I steeled myself. I was aware that the news of Damien's remains being found could come at any moment. It wasn't the outcome that any of us wanted, but we wanted to know *something*. After almost fifteen years of uncertainty, we *needed* to. Not knowing was the very worst torment anyone could go through. If Damien's remains were found, we'd have to accept the heartbreaking fact that he was really gone. But we'd have a body we could lay to rest. We could finally stop searching.

The search pressed on for days. While it was under way DCI Powell called me with some news. My heart had been in my throat when I heard his voice, but he reassured me immediately that Damien hadn't been found.

'We've had an anonymous tip-off,' he said. 'We're going to do some other searches in the area too.' An informant had come forward saying he'd recalled something he'd seen in the days after Damien had gone missing – a man, matching the description of Nicky McNamara, burning clothes in an oil drum outside the chalet. Apparently he'd heard him shouting, 'I am a damned man,' as he'd tossed the clothing into the flames.

The story gripped me with foreboding. Was it just clothes he was burning? *Or . . .*

I squeezed my eyes shut, trying to banish the horrifying thought. I was filled with sadness. My body felt like it was filled with lead, the weight of the vision deeply distressing. Just the idea that this could have been the way my beautiful boy's life might have ended was overwhelming and horrific. How could anybody do such a thing? Part of me wanted to doubt the veracity of the account, but another urged me to leave no stone unturned, no rumour unchallenged. Soon the search team moved on to the new location. It was an old shack owned by a known drug dealer who was allegedly an acquaintance of Nicky McNamara.

Two more people were arrested immediately on suspicion of conspiracy to commit murder: a 35-year-old woman and 44-year-old man from Cowes. Hampshire Constabulary's Major Crime Department, Dog Support Unit, Scientific Services Department and the Island Support Unit searched the ramshackle property intensively. They threw everything at it. But after two days of searching and a total of eight arrests the police had disappointing news for us. Despite all their best efforts, absolutely nothing of any importance was found.

No remains. No new evidence. Nothing.

Five of the people who had been arrested were kept on long-term bail, which meant they had to report for regular bail conditions. Powell put out an appeal for further information and did his best to encourage us to see the positives of the operation. He promised me that he was still determined to find and pursue new leads. But it was little consolation. After weeks of the operation being planned, it was all over much sooner than I expected.

Was that it? I said to myself. There must be more. It couldn't be over, surely? Riding the emotional roller coaster of preparing to be presented with my son's remains, only for that moment never to come, I was relieved and disappointed at the same time. As I was managing to get to grips with these conflicting emotions, a good friend called. The informant who had first told us about the cycle track and Damien's alleged altercation with Nicky had been in touch with her.

'He said they searched the wrong spot,' she said. 'He said Damien was buried in a wooded copse in Gurnard. On GURNARD cycle path.'

It was a place that was also known as the Winding Way. My heart sank. Another fly in the ointment. I was alarmed that the police would have executed their search along the cycle track without making sure it was exactly the right spot the informant was referring to. My friend also told me that the man wasn't just any informant – he had in the past been a long-term police informant. Officers had paid him to give them information about the underworld on the island. I was told the police always trusted his information back in the day. So what had changed?

Once again, I found myself wondering if things had been thoroughly checked. Powell had made a lot of noise about 'getting results' from the start. He'd come in and put the wheels in motion for these searches. But they'd delivered nothing so far. They hadn't even searched all of the locations that had been mentioned. And the ones they had, it seemed they had got wrong. I just wanted to know that nothing was being missed in all the hoo-ha.

I also couldn't help but wonder if it had all been one big PR exercise – a way of putting the case to bed. A big show of force and a swathe of arrests to look like something was getting done? A tick on his checklist to get him out of doing much more on Damien's case?

He had warned me that he would come to a point where there wouldn't be much more he could do.

I was drained, bewildered and angry. But I wasn't going to let them just stop. Not when we had new information that they had searched the wrong site. In the case of this new information, I couldn't ignore what I had heard from my friend. My head said the police must be right. My heart reminded me that Damien was still not found. Experience whispered to me, 'Are they sure they've got the right place?'

I contacted Powell immediately with the information that the wrong location had been searched and demanded that a search of the site in Gurnard be mounted. Much as I expected, my request was refused. He told me in no uncertain terms that the informant had wasted enough police time already. He was clearly exasperated by my demands, but I wanted him to look for my son. We were only struggling now because of the drastic mistakes his predecessors had made. We were still mopping up their mess.

* * *

The activity certainly ruffled a few feathers aside from the police. Although they couldn't be named until an official charge was made, everyone in Cowes and Newport seemed to know exactly whom the suspects were. My email and Facebook inboxes were flooded with messages corroborating theories we'd heard hundreds of times over the years. They also gave an insight into the depths of the relationships between the people arrested and their wider circles.

Even before Damien had gone missing, we'd known that some local families went back generations on the island. But the information I was receiving now, fifteen years on, gave a whole new perspective on some of those family ties. So many of the suspects were intertwined, connected by marriage over the years. There were, of course, many decent, caring people native to our beautiful island who abhorred those who lowered its tone. They were the ones who stood with us. But in that darker circle there were stories of twisted loyalties, cover-ups and vows of silence. All seemingly impenetrable – by us 'overners', at least. It was 'them and us'. Blood was thicker than water. They would protect one another at all costs.

With the suspects on bail and investigations continuing in the background, I knew the police couldn't update me on conversations, but I continued to send them all the information I received in the wake of the operation. One piece of information came via my friend Carmelle. This was from a man who wanted to remain anonymous and called himself 'Mr X'.

Carmelle told me: 'He said that he saw Nicky and some others outside Moira House on Sun Hill, the day after Damien vanished. He said Nicky was putting what appeared to be a bloodied carpet into a red car,' she said. 'He said he jokingly asked them, "What have you got there, a body?" and they all looked at him in horror.' Carmelle said she wasn't sure, but she thought he knew more. 'He's really afraid,' she said.

'I just hope he isn't too scared to tell you more,' I replied. It was another piece of the puzzle we were able to share with the police. I felt like an excited puppy, constantly jumping up at the laps of officers: *Have you checked this out? Have you looked at this? Do you have any news?*

At least this time I was nudging for information on an investigation that was very much active and in progress. Plus, I was certain that some of the snippets I was sharing would be of benefit to the investigation. In the background to all this, an old school friend of Sarah's called Gennive Woolston came up with an idea to raise money for a reward. 'She's going to put on a disco and sell tickets,' Sarah told me on the phone.

'What a lovely idea,' I said.

The kindness of people back on the island always astonished and overwhelmed me. Even after all this time they still thought about us. About Damien. The recent flood of messages from people willing to talk about Damien after the arrests had boosted our confidence. Maybe now enough time had passed for people to no longer fear speaking out?

Perhaps the arrests gave people the confidence to come forward? Or maybe it was people's consciences grinding them down as they looked at their own families and realised what Damien had been deprived of.

What our family had been robbed of.

We were acutely conscious of the same point Ivor had raised when he'd started supporting our efforts – some people would only speak if there was something in it for them. Something more than the relief of a burden or doing the right thing: money. We could be missing out on a whole pool of information without that carrot to dangle.

The police had declined our request to raise a reward fund. They'd seemingly put the blockers on Ivor's approach too. But no one could stop us if we raised the money ourselves.

Gen's idea was perfect. But what started as a simple idea soon snowballed. The fact that the gig supported Damien *and* gave something to the community meant that local businesses and organisations were prepared to offer much more. Everyone wanted to get involved.

Cowes Yacht Haven opened the bar and provided staff for free. Local bands, many friends of Damien, flocked to play. A band called The Zarrs travelled all the way from London to perform. Local TV and radio provided sound technicians and lighting. Each new amazing offer of support was prompted by the previous one. Before she knew it, Gen had a full-scale professional gig on her hands.

'We're calling it "Damien's Gig",' she told me when we spoke one day on the phone. 'It's going to be amazing. It'll raise money *and* awareness.'

'I can't wait to see it,' I told her.

The police had asked me to come over to view their files and reports and wanted to speak to me about the work they had done over the years. I was keen to see this and understand what was going to happen next, but the cost was prohibitive. In the end they offered to pay for me to come over. With a little persuasion from me, they agreed to book the flights for the end of April, so I'd also be there when the gig was taking place. I was truly appreciative of this gesture, as it was important for me to be there.

Over the years, I'd learned that when a person goes missing the focus is automatically on the family, mainly Mum, Dad and brothers and sisters. But what of the friends left behind? Those of the missing person, obviously, but also of their siblings. Having a missing loved one changes a person so completely and profoundly. Friends rally round, but who's there to help those friends deal with such a seismic event? What's more, when a person goes missing their community hurts too. Quietly identifying with the same fear and the emotional distress experienced by the family. Pain spreading like the ripple effect of a stone thrown into a pond.

Like us, they'd never stopped searching for almost sixteen years. They had been as pivotal as us in keeping Damien's memory alive and his case on the police radar. They'd not allowed him to be forgotten about. It was something I never lost sight of. As much as this gig would be for Damien, it would be for them too. For everything they had done and everything we knew they would continue to do.

CHAPTER EIGHTEEN

I N THE MONTHS THAT FOLLOWED THE ARRESTS, WE RECEIVED A DELUGE
of information. Some new, some we'd heard for years. But
the volume was overwhelming. It almost became too much for
me to deal with. There were so many moving pieces:

- Names that recurred but in different scenarios.
- Complex stories of island family loyalties going back
  decades.
- Plausible theories with no evidence.
- Conflicting accounts.
- Stories of corruption, collusion and countless horrific
  crimes that had allegedly occurred over the years on the
  island, at times bordering on the ludicrous.

But some were true. And they'd happened here, where we'd
chosen to bring our kids for a safer, more settled life. I guess
we weren't to know. We probably never would have, had the
unthinkable not happened to our beloved son and brother.

Sleep evaded me as I replayed Mr X's rambling story in my head, wondering if any of what he had told Ivor and Lynn could be true. I wondered if Damien had walked up Sun Hill and come into contact with any of the people Mr X claimed he had seen. He wouldn't give any statement to the police, so his account remained nothing more than speculation. But still, it seeded a thought in my mind.

'Mr X theorised that Damien went into Moira House at the bottom of Sun Hill,' Ivor said, as we discussed the information.

'But why?' I asked.

It seemed very unlikely. But if what Mr X was saying was true, one of the next cameras on Damien's route home – at the bottom of Market Hill or near Bars Hill – would have captured him. 'If we had the CCTV we would be able to check this out properly,' I continued, exasperated.

When I asked the police about this theory, they said that Moira House had been empty for refurbishment at the time. But when Ivor and Lynn started digging around they discovered otherwise.

'Two people have told me they were living there,' Lynn said.

'I've got a lead too,' said Ivor.

As even more accounts poured in, the rest of 'Team Damien' tried to distil the information – to break it down and put it in some kind of order in the hope that the full picture would emerge. But it was like one of those Magic Eye sketches – you could only see it if you were looking at it the right way. But we still didn't know what the 'right way' was.

You'd have thought we'd be at the point of giving up. But the funny thing about adversity is that it taps into reserves of strength you never knew you had. No matter how overwhelming and confusing things got we never for a second thought about giving up. Our family was stronger than ever. United by our one missing piece. Our Damien.

With speculation at the highest I'd ever known it, the media's interest was once again piqued. It wasn't only due to our efforts raising a new reward fund. They were hearing new stories on the grapevine too. I couldn't help but wonder what whispers we hadn't heard yet, especially as we always seemed to be the last to know about certain things. Like police officers changing jobs . . .

I received an email from DI Sharon Murray, an officer who had been working on Damien's case alongside DCI Powell. She spotted somewhere that the Missing People charity had suggested suspects had been charged in relation to Damien's disappearance and she wanted me to ask them to correct the statement.

'DCI Powell asked me to make contact on his behalf, as he is very busy with his new job at the moment,' she said.

New job?

I emailed back confirming that I would speak to the charity, and also expressing my surprise at Powell's news. He'd made us aware that he wouldn't be SIO forever, but it worried me that he'd taken this new role at such a sensitive time for the case.

Murray replied and explained Powell *was* still Damien's SIO, but alongside his new role. She did her best to reassure me, saying she was on Damien's case full-time and that nothing would change. By now I knew how this went. I was disappointed, but it was nothing compared to what we felt when we received Powell's next update on the arrests.

Four of the men who had been arrested were to be released

without charge. There hadn't been enough evidence to tie them to Damien's disappearance. Almost sixteen years on from when Damien had first vanished, I was starting to feel that our chances were slipping away. It made a hard year even more difficult.

In the coming November I would have spent longer *without* Damien in my life than I'd had him in it. It was inconceivable to think; almost like another form of bereavement. Grief over a life that I didn't share. The case was so old now that I wondered how much more we'd be able to do. How much longer we could hold people's interest.

I'd been pushing Powell to facilitate a *Crimewatch* feature, to drive awareness further afield. Maybe someone who'd lived on the island in 1996 but had since moved away might hold some vital information? But DCI Powell steadfastly refused to push this idea. He said Damien's case didn't fit the *Crimewatch* criteria, as there was no known crime. So why had cases similar to Damien's been featured over the years? In the face of my protests, Powell was unmoved. He said it would be more hindrance than help. Open the floodgates to too much unhelpful information. *Or did he mean too much extra work?*

Despite once again hitting that big blue wall, I was determined to fight on. However, the worry of Damien's story falling off people's radars began to affect my judgement. Maybe it was an element of panic simmering under the surface – fearfulness that if the spotlight turned away again, it wouldn't come back. That, combined with changes on Damien's case team and trying to deal with all the stories that were coming to us through Facebook and Ivor and Lynn, meant that somehow I let my guard down a little.

I'd always been clear that I didn't think Damien had been

'involved' in drugs. He may well have smoked pot, if it had been accessible to him, but I believed that he and his friends had been much more interested in buying cigarettes and cider. Yet in recent months we'd heard more vague rumours about a local thug with connections to drug dealing being spotted holding a youth up against a wall at the corner of Bars Hill after midnight. I uncomfortably wondered if this could have been Damien. It tallied with other reports of noise of a fight after the last sighting of him on the CCTV. There was the claim by Mr X that Nicky McNamara had been in town.

It wasn't outside the realms of possibility . . .

With all this fresh in my mind, I let my guard down in an interview with the BBC. I said a little too much about some of the stories spinning round my head. I mentioned that I was worried Damien had got in the way of the wrong kind of people on the night he vanished – the drug dealers and thugs that had plagued the island at that time. When the story was published, I was horrified by the headline: MOTHER OF DAMIEN NETTLES TALKS OF DRUGS DEBT MURDER THEORY.

While the quotes attributed to me accurately reflected what I'd said, the opening line made me wince: 'The mother of missing Isle of Wight teenager Damien Nettles has described how she believes her son was murdered over a cannabis debt.'

I had said those words. Those possibilities were in my head but there was no factual evidence. But I'd never expressly said that I thought Damien was killed over a drug debt. To me, that inferred a deeper connection between the sweet boy I knew and these thugs. I was angrier with myself than the journalist. I should have known how this worked by now. Our relationships with newspapers and news sites, TV and radio stations had always been largely positive, and I believed wholeheartedly that many supported us in our fight. But we were aware the relationship was mutually beneficial. We gave them snippets of newsworthy information to make people read their publication. They gave us vital exposure for Damien's case. But I was now learning that some were simply keen for a salacious story, whether or not it was factual.

Inevitably local media like the *Isle of Wight County Press* picked up on the BBC story and did their own follow-up with me. I did my best to clarify what I'd actually said to the BBC but, with the story out there in the public domain, it was like shutting the stable door after the horse had bolted. In the end I decided to take it on the chin and put it down to experience. As well as the salacious side of the story, all of the media had published details of 'Damien's Gig' and our fundraising appeal for a reward fund. That was the pay-off. You give a little to get a little.

While all this was going on, Murray kept me up to date on progress with the suspects who had been kept on bail. She maintained the same level of contact we'd come to expect from Powell. They were still struggling to pin down anything that would convince the Crown Prosecution Service to allow the force to charge them. Powell also emailed me with some updates.

'It doesn't make for good reading in providing you with any answers,' he began in one email, before outlining where they were up to with each lead I had passed on to them. His summary continued: 'There have been numerous people who have been adamant that they know what has happened to Damien, but when really tested, their information is without foundation.'

I was deflated but not entirely surprised. So many people had been so willing to talk, but the moment the police became involved they'd denied their stories, lacked information or simply gone to ground. Scattered like sewer rats. I did believe that the police were pushing as hard as they could on those who had been arrested and their associates. But when it came to new leads and opportunities, I wasn't so sure. We'd made repeated requests for the police to put up a reward for information but they had refused, to much local outcry.

What's more, as well as learning that the wrong cycle path had apparently been searched, and by identifying the correct one, we'd also been given information from other sources that Damien's body may have been buried in Parkhurst Forest. We'd urged the police to look at both seriously, but they refused. They insisted that the site they searched was the one that they had been shown by the informant. Who was I supposed to believe? And how could they expect me to leave it alone?

We remained determined to find something that would jolt them into action. If that meant us raising a reward fund alone, then so be it. We hoped that 'Damien's Gig' would give the fund a kick-start. Ahead of the event I spoke frankly to the *County Press* about Damien's upcoming anniversary.

'No parent should have to be asking the question, "Where's my child's body?"' I said. 'Sixteen years is the kicker for me. I had him sixteen years and he'll have been gone sixteen years in November. That's going to be a difficult one but we'll get through it, I'm sure.'

We'd got through everything else.

* * *

When I arrived back on the island, I met with my brother Nigel to attend the case review meeting. It was different to other meetings we'd had before. Usually it was just our SIO and maybe one other in a poky meeting room in Cowes Police Station. But this time it was at Hampshire Police HQ, in Fratton, Portsmouth. We were taken to a room with DCI Powell, DI Larry Grist and DI Sharon Murray. There were stacks of case files and a wall filled with names and pictures, like you'd see in incident rooms on police TV programmes. It was impressive, imposing even.

'Think of the money sitting around this table today,' Nigel whispered to me, referring to the salaries of the officers in the room and the time they were devoting to this meeting in the midst of their other demands.

'I know,' I replied, with a hint of suspicion. 'I wonder what they're going to say.'

'We want to take you through everything we have done,' said DCI Powell. 'From the very start right up to the present day.'

DI Dave Steel, who had been an officer on the case at the time Damien disappeared, was now head of the search team. He said they didn't usually bring him into meetings like this, but they had made an exception for us. If it was meant to make an impression, it did all right. But only because one of the first things out of his mouth was completely inaccurate. He said that on the day the police had come to the house with their colleagues to speak to us, a thorough search had been undertaken.

'No it wasn't,' I said immediately.

'Pardon?' Steel said.

'There was no thorough search. They looked briefly in Damien's room and an officer went up into the loft with Ed,' I said. I remembered it as plain as day. To me a 'thorough search' meant taking beds apart and emptying cupboards. None of that had happened.

'Er, well, I see,' said Steel. 'We're just going on notes from the time.'

'Well, they are incorrect,' I said.

'We'll take a look into that for you,' Powell interjected. I wanted to ensure they knew that I was very aware of what had *not* been done. I'd been searching for my boy long enough to see through all that.

After several hours they'd covered off everything, but I was still not clear where the investigation was going next. Truth be told, it made me wonder if they had anything else planned at all. I was glad I had the gig to look forward to.

Thankfully that was a roaring success, raising around £1,500 for the reward fund and bringing the total raised to £3,000. If I'd only come to the island for the review, I would have considered it a fairly pointless and disappointing trip. But it felt amazing to see so many people turning out for Damien. Some I knew well; others who simply followed us on Facebook came over to introduce themselves to me in person. It was heartening and humbling all at the same time. The community coming together for a good cause: for our Damien.

We were riding high after the gig, confident we'd be able to generate more money for the reward fund. Nigel and his wife Janet arranged an open-house tour of his historical property in Gloucester, accompanied by fresh tea and scones, raising a further £1,000. We were also pinning our hopes on good news about the suspects who remained on bail: the man from Ryde, who was arrested on suspicion of murder, and two people who had been taken in on suspicion of conspiracy to murder after a raid on a chalet in Marsh Road. All three were due to answer bail on 7 June 2012.

The wait was agonising, but we finally received the news. It was not what we had wanted to hear. All three had been released without charge. I then experienced a feeling of crushing disappointment that words couldn't even begin to describe.

Powell had always been clear that despite all best efforts he might not be able to prove anything. In the logical corner of my brain, I understood that. But he was speaking to the desperate mother of a missing boy. Pragmatism went straight out of the window, overpowered by my maternal urge to find my missing child. Plus, the blunders over the years always left me in doubt that everything had been done effectively. He could talk until he was blue in the face. He could lay out all the possibilities. But if there was any glimmer of hope, I would only ever hear one thing: *maybe we can find Damien now.*

Calling round the family to let them know the news sapped every last bit of energy out of me. Hearing the shock and anger in their voices as I delivered the news shattered me. I felt every last one of their emotions. We'd all truly felt that we were getting somewhere. But now we were back to square one all over again.

CHAPTER NINETEEN

WE WEREN'T THE ONLY ONES WHO WERE DEALT A BLOW BY THE release of the suspects. Nor were we the only people confused and alarmed by the police's refusal to search Parkhurst Forest and the other site in Gurnard. Our informant was livid too. He remained absolutely adamant that Damien would be found on the cycle path in Gurnard. Not the cycle track in Newport that had been searched by police.

'I told them Gurnard,' he said. 'They got it wrong!' He'd gone into more detail about what he knew as well. 'I saw the sail bag that Damien was moved in,' he said. 'It was at a house on Fellows Road. A dealer called Bunny Iles rented a room there.'

My ears pricked up. Bunny Iles was a name that had started cropping up in the stories we heard.

'They'd been showing me stolen goods they had in bags. When I went to look in the sail bag they stopped me,' he said. Apparently one of the men there had smirked and said: 'You don't want to look in there.'

Our informant even told of young boys who had drug debts. They'd been roped in to dispose of his body. One of them had been sobbing apparently because he'd seen Damien's murder. 'The kids had no choice,' he said. 'They had debts to pay.'

I gasped. Not only because the idea chilled me to my core, but also because it unearthed a memory from years back – an anonymous message through the website that described something vey similar. It had sounded horrific and implausible at the time. So implausible that I'd forgotten it until this moment. But that was before all the information about the island's drug fraternity and Nicky McNamara had come to light. Now it seemed no less horrific but entirely possible.

Surely the easiest way to find out would be to dig all the sites we had been pointed to? Like a dog with a bone, Ivor persisted and even went directly to the Forestry Commission to see if they would grant permission for us to dig in Parkhurst Forest. But with the police refusing to declare it a crime scene, they declined our request. If we even tried it we would risk being arrested.

As a family, we were at a loss. Powell was committed to his decision not to dig any site. Instinct told us to take matters into our own hands; go down there with torches and shovels and dig the spot ourselves. But where would we start, Gurnard or Parkhurst Forest?

Which account did we think was the most plausible?

Then, of course, there was the moral question. Did we go digging where we had expressly been told not to – on someone else's property and against all advice? As desperate as we were, our family was a good, upstanding bunch. We didn't want to lower ourselves to breaking the law or getting other good people into trouble. We knew Damien wouldn't want that either.

With Parkhurst Forest off limits, we decided to focus on the copse near Gurnard cycle path. The police had washed their hands of it saying our informant was a time-waster. But as it was on private land they couldn't stop us from searching ourselves. Not if we had the permission of the landowner. Sarah made contact and amazingly he not only granted us permission, he joined in on the dig too. 'Team Damien', as we now called ourselves, swung into action. Lynn, and our friends Kaley Hall and Paula Hall, searched the area whenever time allowed. They didn't want to attract attention, after all.

'What if the police ask you what you're up to?' I asked one of the team.

'We say we're helping to clear some space for the landowner,' she said with a smile.

Our small-scale efforts would take time, we knew. But we put everything we could into it. We even managed to get some guys with a digger to help us. We weren't going to give up. The digging debate was just one we continued to have with the police. The other was regarding remains and bodies that turned up on the island.

Until proven otherwise, there was still every chance they could be Damien's. Quite often we'd first hear about them from people on the island, rather than the police. This lack of 'heads up' about new finds never became any less aggravating for the family. When new remains washed up, we tried to function productively in our day-to-day lives as employees, parents and partners, but pure focus on anything was impossible. It wasn't so much the waiting; it was the way it was handled. It always felt like we were the last to know.

Unimportant and forgotten.

I guess for that reason I shouldn't have been surprised when I got wind of a police search taking place in none other than Parkhurst Forest. The news came from an associate of Ivor's. Police activity had been noticed at the Noke Common entrance to the forest. The same spot that had been identified as a potential gravesite for Damien.

Years of experience had told us not to jump to conclusions. One account could sometimes just be rumour. But then we had a second. And a third. Had they finally found solid evidence they were willing to act on? At this point I called Hampshire Constabulary. I was hoping to speak to Powell, but he wasn't around, so I asked the officer on the line.

'Is this search in relation to Damien?' I asked, filled with a heady mix of concern and hope.

'No, Mrs Nettles, it's unrelated,' the officer said. Once again I was deflated. All of our recent pleas to the police had focused on getting a search in this area. If it was unrelated, why hadn't we been warned, so we didn't get our hopes up unnecessarily? I emailed Powell to express our family's distress. According to him he was still both my SIO and FLO, so he was the most appropriate person to contact about this.

I knew there was a chance that he hadn't been aware of the search, but he wasn't the only officer on Damien's case who knew what effect this sort of thing had on our family. Not to mention how locals would jump to the same conclusions. The police weren't a counselling service – that we understood – but a little consideration really wouldn't hurt.

'It should not have taken much imagination by officers to have figured out how this might look to locals and that we would hear about this activity,' I said.

I received an email apology from Powell that same day. He said the search was conducted by another police force, not Hampshire. He'd only found out about it himself as it happened. He told me that he had asked for me to be contacted, but regrettably that had not happened.

I took the explanation with a pinch of salt. It seemed odd for the police not to communicate with one another when coming into another force's territory. I felt like we had just been forgotten. Again. Once in a while would be understandable, but with us it seemed to happen with frustrating regularity. Eventually we found out that the search uncovered a hidden arms cache that had potentially been left by the IRA. Some of the toughest members of their organisation had been incarcerated in HMP Parkhurst over the years. The irony was that one of the reasons police had given for not searching the forest was that it was too difficult for anyone to get into it.

So who had buried those arms?

It was yet another cruel disappointment for us.

CHAPTER TWENTY

WE WERE DUE SOME GOOD NEWS AND, IN OCTOBER 2012, IT came. Hampshire Constabulary told us it was willing to raise a £20,000 reward fund for any information that could potentially lead to the discovery of Damien's body and the conviction of the perpetrator. For what had felt like an eternity I'd pressed the police to raise a reward, but I'd always been refused, so when the news came it was a welcome surprise. It wasn't a life-changing amount, but it was the carrot on a stick that we had always wanted to dangle but had never quite been able to raise ourselves, despite all of the best efforts of our supporters.

For years we had watched as tens of thousands of pounds were pumped into searches for British missing people in Greece and Portugal. Wonderful for those families, but there was never a penny for our Damien. Or other families of the missing living in limbo on British soil.

Obviously we were over the moon when we found out. We learned that the reward would remain in place until April

2013, after which the situation would be reviewed. Still riding the wave of speculation from the arrests and various searches, I hoped it would keep up momentum. Nudge those people willing to speak just a little more.

But our excitement was tinged with sadness and frustration. Why hadn't they done this sixteen years ago? If they had then maybe we wouldn't have had all this anguish and torment. Maybe they wouldn't have had us knocking on their door daily, making their lives difficult. At least that's how it felt.

The media flew into a frenzy and I was bombarded with requests for interviews. By now I had developed my own sense of loyalty with the media, and I went to the Isle of Wight's local media first. Damien once again made front-page news. I'd always imagined he might, as I watched him grow up, but not for this reason. Maybe as a rock star, or for making an amazing discovery as a marine biologist. But the headline said everything that I wanted people on the island to know: £20,000 REWARD TO TRACK DOWN DAMIEN.

The police had told the journalist they hadn't been under pressure to put up a reward from us, but rather it had been designed to maximise opportunities for new information as Damien's anniversary approached. I smiled and shook my head in dismay at the suggestion that we hadn't put pressure on them. And the idea that it was a strategic move? What about the fifteen other anniversaries that had come before this one? Our own fundraising efforts and public perception about the case had forced their hand, more likely. But I let it slide. What was happening was a positive and I had to be thankful for it. I had to hope that this would bring us our resolution. Bring Damien home so we could grieve.

In every media interview I made it abundantly clear that, over the years, I had learned how some elements of the island worked back then and how they still did today. I made it clear what we were hoping for.

'Sixteen years ago there were a lot of loyalties in the community that perhaps would have prohibited people from wanting to come forward and speak up about what they know,' I told the BBC. 'Maybe now old loyalties have dwindled and fizzled out. This could be an incentive for those people. It's not too late.'

It was my best hope. At the same time DCI Powell was making his expectations clear.

'I stress that speculation, gossip and the spreading of rumours won't help the police and the Nettles family find the answers we seek in this investigation,' he'd said to the *County Press*. He wanted secure, reliable evidence, and the clock was ticking.

A week passed and information began to come in. We weren't privy to everything, and we knew that every account needed to be addressed methodically and properly investigated, but the island grapevine kept us well informed. Once again a towering high was followed by a devastating thud back down to earth.

More information did come through, however, suggesting that Damien had been seen shouting up at the flat above the butcher's. Over the years, rumour had indicated that two men with drug-related criminal histories were living in the flat. Both had made statements saying they were in the flat that night. A third man was allegedly there too: Nicky McNamara. Right in the heart of the action again.

Since we'd first heard it, the story had expanded. Damien was apparently heard shouting to someone to 'throw something down'. I know that people assumed Damien knew who was up there, and that he was calling out for drugs, but I had another theory. You see, Damien had grown up in New Orleans. During Mardi Gras, as the parade of floats passes by, it is traditional to appeal for 'throws' – strings of coloured beads stamped with the name of the group who had made that float. The shout was always the same: 'Throw me something, mister!'

I knew Damien's loud, silly sense of humour. I knew that he didn't always know when to rein it in. And I knew full well that people didn't always appreciate it as much as we did.

Drunk, and in good spirits, had he seen someone in a window and played the joker? Had he drawn attention to Nicky when he was trying to stay off the radar?

We also heard again that people living in homes off The Parade, not far from Bars Hill, had reported shouting, almost like a fight taking place, sometime after midnight. Understanding now where CCTV cameras in the Bath Road area had been positioned, I realised that one of the tapes could have confirmed or dismissed this rumour with ease. But that wasn't possible, was it? Because Hampshire Constabulary had lost all that footage early in the investigation. Kilbride had been right – that CCTV would indeed have been a gift. But the police had failed miserably to protect the evidence. It galled me that everything seemed to come back to this. Their sheer incompetence had resulted in a life of limbo for our family. The footage on just one tape might have put an end to our misery. But that wasn't our lot.

With Damien's sixteenth anniversary around the corner, we relaunched the billboard campaign in Newport, supported again by friends and local businesses. Perhaps the addition of a juicy reward would have a greater impact?

Kaley arranged a peaceful march through Newport in December 2012 to raise awareness of the reward and possible burial sites for Damien. After hearing that the police had refused to dig the sites, she'd been compelled to take action. The march focused on highlighting three sites – two specific locations in Parkhurst Forest and the cycle path in Gurnard. The police had looked at the evidence to support all three and still refused to search. The information wasn't good enough, apparently. Even with the reward in place, the police made constant caveats to us and to the public. They were like a broken record.

The crucial challenge in this case is separating fact from fiction. Only facts will allow our enquiries to locate Damien.

Gossip and rumours won't help.

Quite frankly it left us wondering what *would* be good enough. I was beyond infuriated with their attitude. This mess was their own doing. They had created this situation and left massive holes in it. That was how it got filled with rumour and speculation. What they dismissed as gossip was a possibility not to be missed, in my book. On the surface it looked like the police were doing what was expected of them when it came to facilitating a peaceful protest. However, I learned from those organising the march that it had been anything but plain sailing. It felt like the police would have preferred to shut it down.

Reading between the lines of their statements published in the media, I could see what they were trying to do. When they referenced the Parkhurst Forest sites we wanted them to dig, there was a casual mention that some of the information had come from a séance. It was true. A well-meaning group of amateur mediums from the island had reached out to me with some information that had come from one of their gatherings. But it was just one of many accounts pointing to the forest. They were trying to discredit us. Make us look wacky. Well, we weren't. There was a lot more behind the forest information than that séance, and they knew it.

Although I couldn't be at the march, I decided to make my own intentions and feelings clear. I drew on that strength inside me that had flourished over the years and I let loose. Never in a thousand lifetimes did I think I would be making defiant statements aimed at my local police force, but when I spoke to a reporter from the news site, On the Wight, ahead of the march, that was exactly what I did.

'I will be relentless in my search and will not take no for an answer when it comes to my son. I will take as long as it takes or I have breath in my body,' I said, speaking with fire in my belly. 'I will take on all those "suits" who hide behind the badges and the titles and I will make them hear me!'

Dozens of our supporters marched peacefully from Cineworld in Newport, through town, ending up at Newport Police Station opposite County Hall. I was certain that the message would have been heard loud and clear. Afterwards, everyone went to the Hogshead pub for some well-deserved refreshments. As the event organiser, Kaley was mingling with participants and chatting to the people who had marched. An elderly man wearing a hearing aid, who was also sitting in the pub, walked across to speak to her.

'Isn't it a shame he was never found?' the man said. 'I was in the chip shop that night.' He'd spotted the posters and had been compelled to come over.

She shared the conversation with me later that day via text. As she described the conversation, I suddenly twigged something. I recalled a moment in the CCTV footage from Yorkies, when a man with white hair entered the chip shop. He stood in the queue for a minute and then left. Like the other men in the chip shop, we had never been able to identify him. I couldn't help but wonder what he'd overheard. Kaley hadn't been aware of this connection, so she hadn't taken the man's details. She and another friend immediately set about looking him up.

It wasn't the only piece of information to emerge from the march. A lady who had worked at the Harbour Lights pub when Damien disappeared approached Kaley.

'I might have been one of the last people to see him alive, you know,' she said. 'Outside the pub on the night he went missing.'

When Kaley told me this I gasped audibly. I knew immediately who *this* was. When Corran and I had been pounding the streets in the days after Damien disappeared, we'd gone into the Harbour Lights with his photograph. This lady had been working behind the bar.

'She told me that she hadn't seen him,' I said, as I explained to Kaley. 'I showed her Damien's picture and she shook her head.'

'Really?' she asked.

'Yes,' I said firmly. I remembered it as clear as day. 'Her colleague followed me out after I left the pub and said she thought she might have been mistaken, but then nothing came of it.'

I was stunned and baffled. Why say this now, so many years on? Why didn't she tell me at the time? How could we possibly keep track of all these moving pieces and create any sort of picture if people kept misinforming us?

After the success of the march, the year ended with fresh

uncertainty. Kaley eventually tracked down the old man, and DI Grist visited him accompanied by another officer. He was greeted by the man's brother, who denied it was him in the footage. He said he was suffering poor mental health and that he didn't recall saying he was in Yorkies that night. We still felt it was odd he'd come forward in a busy pub to speak to Kaley, but the police dismissed the lead. They said the man must have overheard what was being said. But he was in a loud pub, and deaf, so how could that be? It was yet another hope dashed.

As for the barmaid, after I passed on what she'd said to the police, she was re-interviewed, but nothing came of it. She claimed that we must have been mistaken or misinterpreted what she'd said. I was furious that yet another 'witness' wasn't willing to put their money where their mouth was.

DCI Powell confirmed to us once again that the police commitment to the case was undiminished, but he also advised us that the reward would not run past its expiry date in April 2013, despite our requests for an extension. He also continued to refuse to dig the three sites the march had served to highlight. What's more, in the three months since the reward had been offered, only twenty pieces of new information had been forthcoming. I was disappointed, but at least it had been tried. Perhaps it would have been more fruitful if the reward had been in place in 1996 – way before Damien became an urban legend that everyone claimed some connection to.

I could feel time slipping away from us. This time I feared it would be our very last chance to get justice for Damien.

CHAPTER TWENTY-ONE

EVERY DAY WAS LIKE WATCHING SAND SLIP THROUGH AN HOURGLASS. Each grain representing a chance to find out what happened to Damien that we couldn't get back. It was agonising. We did what we could to continue to promote the reward, and remind people there was still time to speak up. Our local media, as ever, rallied with us.

According to the police, they had investigated all viable leads and none of the evidence was reliable enough. One missing boy. Hundreds of statements. Yet not one credible witness? I couldn't help but wonder if there were other forces at work. Were people being warned off coming forward? After the chilling incident at The Anchor gig a few years earlier, we'd also learned that someone who attended the séance that pointed us to Parkhurst Forest had also been approached and warned off. The poor thing had been so scared she'd refused to speak to police. Were we getting too close for comfort after all these years?

Looking at all the threads of theories, the snippets of

information and the hearsay, it didn't feel that way to us. But to a guilty party all the activity might be somewhat unnerving.

Or maybe so much time had passed that people couldn't remember or maybe didn't even care anymore?

So much time had passed, in fact, that some of the suspects in the case and even the names that popped up in connection to it, had died. That, combined with the expiry date for the reward moving ever closer, tied knots in my stomach. We were losing ground from all angles. It would have been easy to crumble. Say it was 'game over' and admit defeat. But as long as Damien wasn't found, that wouldn't happen. I had to try and stay a little bit hopeful.

Ivor passed on every snippet of information he got to DCI Powell and his team. I asked again and again for the reward deadline to be extended. We could be just one piece of information away from cracking the case. Everything I shared, however, seemed to be thrown out as unreliable or not worth consideration – even one statement given to Ivor that I felt tied into so much other information we already had. An unsigned statement provided by the notorious Shirley Barrett.

She denied having anything to do with Damien's disappearance but she did say that Nicky McNamara had picked Damien up with another man whom she refused to name, on the night he vanished. She claimed he had picked him up on the Cowes end of Baring Road, not far from Bars Hill. It wasn't a million miles from where Simon W, who'd contacted me when the police searched Gurnard back in 1998, had placed Damien all those years ago. The police spoke to Shirley, but it amounted to nothing.

As the deadline approached we were all truly despondent. All hope crushed by the lack of any real progress, despite so much opportunity and effort. The island underworld remained silent, while rumours rumbled around its coastline. If the offer of £20,000 wasn't sufficient to get people to talk, what would be? In April, the police confirmed our worst fears: the reward deadline would not be extended. I was dumbfounded, disappointed and disillusioned. With nothing to tempt people to speak, with no new leads and a case that was now firmly embedded in urban myth, I was sure this would be the end of the road. Where else did we have to go?

When the news was released, the police said that the case would be reviewed but remained open. For now, I thought. Would the next 'review' lead to Damien's case being marked a cold case? I wasn't completely sure of the criteria, but I was betting we weren't far off. As I pondered on the limited success of the reward, I wondered if the time frame had ever been long enough. With the family ties and loyalties on the island, was six months really long enough to turn in a close friend or relative to the police, possibly incriminating yourself in the process? I very much doubted it.

In all honesty, I also couldn't help but feel that some of the police activity over the past couple of years had been a little disingenuous. It was as if they had taken two years to fix all the mistakes and unaddressed issues spanning sixteen years. Now they were hoping to draw some kind of a line under the case. Allowing them to put it on a shelf to gather dust, under the guise of being open. But not really working on it. Because, hey, what else could they do?

* * *

After the reward was removed I felt bereft again. The feeling of failure and no way forward weighed heavily on me. For over sixteen years I had ploughed on and on, always finding a new way forward, but now I had no idea what to do. I *had* to keep on searching for my Damien. But how? Everything I thought of we'd already tried, or didn't have police support for. It was like I was in a pitch-black room grasping desperately for a door handle. A way out. A way back to the light, where I could see more clearly.

We reopened our own fund, which had remained suspended for the duration of the police's campaign, and started appealing for donations again. We continued tirelessly, campaigning, digging and running events while continuing to maintain a high presence on social media. Facebook had become a remarkable asset for us and we weren't about to let activity dip there. But it all felt so futile, and we were truly at our lowest point. Until one day the light we were searching for came to us.

A local businessman approached Sarah and offered us £10,000 to be used as a reward for further information. More than that, if that failed, he promised to pay for a specialist dog team to search locations on the island. I could have leapt into the air with joy. Damien's campaign had been thrown a lifeline. We were back in business!

When I finally made direct contact with the businessman, on a Project Damien text message thread, I was overwhelmed. Once again I was seeing the very best of human nature. True kindness.

'We're so grateful for your support,' I said, 'But why are you doing this for us?' We'd wanted to thank him publicly, but he'd asked to remain anonymous from the get-go. So it wasn't for personal gain or publicity. *So why?*

'I read something Sarah wrote on Facebook,' he said. 'She was talking about Damien and the man that he could have been. It choked me up.'

I knew exactly which post he meant, as I'd cried myself when I'd read it. The man continued: 'I cannot think of anything worse than what you've been through. I know all you want is to get him back,' he said. 'I'm fortunate enough to be in a position to help you with that.'

'I really don't know how to thank you,' I said.

'You don't need to,' he replied.

We'll find you yet, Damien, I whispered to myself.

The businessman advertised the reward in all the local newspapers and launched a brand-new billboard campaign. This time it was to be towed on the back of a truck around the island. During Cowes Week, the island's annual regatta, it was even situated in the car park at Northwood Park. He wanted maximum impact to promote the reward. The poster read: 'If you were not there on the night Damien Nettles was buried then you can stop reading this, move on and enjoy your day.' The implication being, if you were, get in touch.

The wording on the poster went on to explain that the new reward would also be available to anonymous claimants giving solid information about the precise location of Damien's body, not who was responsible for his suspected murder. The businessman even set up an email address containing the words 'precise location'. No charges would be brought; we just wanted to know where he lay. So we could bring him home.

After so many years, we still didn't know if Damien had been killed, but I no longer wanted to know who might be responsible. I was tired. I wanted to know where my son was. I wanted a marker. A place where I could visit. To be near him.

It was a completely different approach to the police campaign and we hoped it would encourage people to come forward and tell us where Damien was. Of course, Hampshire Constabulary had an opinion on the news; they even issued a statement. As I read it in the local paper, my blood positively boiled: 'We must remain mindful that the 30 pieces of information received in response to a £20,000 police reward only repeated previous unfounded speculation, contained factually inaccurate details, or fell short of police standards for a reliable source.'

Although they would argue differently, it smacked of them saying that nothing that came from our new lifeline would be good enough. We'd never get what they wanted. Well, we were sure that our lucrative offer, given time, would bring us the answers we'd been longing for. The reward was offered initially for six weeks. We waited eagerly for any information to come in.

It wasn't the deluge we'd perhaps expected. A few bits of interest came in, which we passed on to the police. One piece was particularly compelling. A cyclist had apparently recalled disturbing a group of men, who looked like they were up to no good, on the cycle track between Cowes and Gurnard. It was the opposite end to where the police searches had taken place, but still an area of interest. The information was compelling enough for the businessman to decide to keep the reward open for a little longer. But after a few more weeks, nothing, and no one else was forthcoming. The reward was withdrawn in mid-October 2013.

I couldn't help but think that the wall of silence was down to everything we knew so far, everything we had learned and the places we were looking at. We were close, but the drugs fraternity on the island was shutting down. Were they fearful of being caught? Or what might happen to them if they 'snitched'? Or was there no connection there at all? We were pulled apart with all these theories. By the time this reward period ended, there was still nothing that contained credible enough evidence to justify the police performing a full-scale search and recovery operation.

Once again the fragile framework of my existence was shattered. We were plummeted back into a black hole. I didn't know how much more I could take. But I couldn't get off this roller coaster, with heady heights and devastating lows. Not until I brought my boy back home.

CHAPTER TWENTY-TWO

THE 'DIGS FOR DAMIEN' CONTINUED IN THE COPSE IN GURNARD well into 2014. Despite many requests, the police refused to investigate or even offer support. When any items of interest were found, we informed our latest SIO, DI Liz Williams (another Williams), and asked for officers to be sent out to look at them. But they rarely attended.

It was only now I realised what had really happened in that flashy review meeting back in 2012. They'd been winding down. It hadn't sunk in at the time, but looking back I could see it was one last fickle fanfare before they could at last box up Damien's case and put it on a shelf to gather dust. I think it only really hit home when 'Team Damien' stumbled upon a truly gruesome find. A white, waxy substance about six foot underground in the area where they had been digging. One of the volunteers helping to dig that day was a nurse and she'd spotted it straight away.

'She said it looked like something called adipocere,' Lynn

said. 'Apparently this was often found at sites where a body had been lying for some time.' *Like eighteen years . . .*

'My goodness,' I exclaimed. I never in my life thought I'd hear such a thing. But here I was, Googling the word to find out more. Apparently it was more commonly known as 'death wax'. It had particular properties, like not dissolving when put in water. I was alarmed to find out that when the dig team tested it in water, it stayed just as it was. We reported the find to the police immediately.

DI Liz Williams eventually came to the site with a forensics person, but there was no follow-up. When I wrote to her to voice my concerns, I was told that she was trying to 'get permission' to test selected items that had been found at the dig site, including the potential 'death wax'. But almost at the same time, my concerns about the substance were brushed off. I was told that if it were adipoccre there would be bones in the vicinity too. My frustration levels once again soared sky high. *This was why we wanted a proper search!* There was concrete in the site that our team couldn't get through alone. How were we supposed to know there weren't any bones in there if we didn't look? We needed specialist equipment and manpower for that, which the police wouldn't give us.

Another year, another glaring missed opportunity.

It took about a month for the force to finally and bluntly come back with news that the substance we'd found hadn't been 'death wax', but they didn't tell us what it was. In fact, we hadn't even known that the testing had taken place.

I'd like to say we were back to square one, but in reality it felt like we were so much further back than that. The case remained open, but it most certainly wasn't active in my book. Our family remained in limbo. One foot in the present. One back in 1996. It would always be the way until we brought Damien home.

In time, the 'Digs for Damien' became less frequent. Our committed and well-intentioned supporters had lives to get on with and the activity gradually fizzled out. Sarah tried to continue to rally support, writing an appeal for volunteers to join the digging effort once a month, but to little avail. I had no doubt that she meant the final words in her appeal: 'We are not giving up or giving in.'

But where were we to go from here? What was our next best hope? This time there didn't seem to be one. Ivor's involvement, the two consecutive rewards – each had been unexpected blessings, although we still had no answers. But there was nothing on the horizon this time. I couldn't even conceive what else could be done. It felt like we'd truly exhausted all of our options. It wasn't that we'd suddenly found ourselves short of information. It was support in sorting the wheat from the chaff that was lacking. The fact from the fiction. The stories still trickled in, but unless it was brand new and compelling evidence from a credible source, the police wouldn't touch it.

I understood both sides of the argument, but to me nothing should be too much effort to find my boy. It was so frustrating when we did hear things that we thought could be of interest, like when Ivor and Lynn had spoken to Mr X again and he'd provided even more detail about the night that Damien disappeared.

By this time Ivor had been off the scene for over a year, after falling ill with some very serious health issues that had almost claimed his life, but we still had the information he'd gleaned previously to consider. I recalled the information from Mr X that he'd shared before he became unwell.

'He said that he saw Nicky McNamara and his posse coming down Sun Hill between 11:30pm and 11:40pm on the night Damien vanished. He told me he spoke to him,' Ivor had told me. 'He said Nicky seemed off his face on something and was spinning round, doing "windmills" with his arms. He named a few of the other people there too. They all had connections to local thugs and dealers. There was a really tall woman and a few men. One of them was the dealer called Bunny Iles. Notorious fella.'

So I'd heard. The list of convictions he had for drugs-related offences was eye-watering. Apparently he and Nicky had been real brothers in arms. The cogs in my brain started turning. Could the tall woman have been Shirley Barrett? We knew she moved in these circles and she'd ended up in a relationship with Nicky years later, so it wasn't inconceivable they might've been friends back then. Also, these people had been rolling through town just as my Damien had been there. Did they cross paths? If Mr X's account was right, then Nicky must have left the flat above the butcher's at some point. Maybe he had gone to meet up with his cronies? Once again we were trying to put together what we'd heard – the continual stream of theories and whispers – and make it fit. To try and make some sense out of it.

He'd shared some other snippets too, about speaking to a policeman just as he'd bumped into Nicky McNamara, noting the heavy police presence in town. When I spoke to the police, they said this wasn't the case. Apparently Mr X had spoken to them about everything back in 2011, but he'd refused to sign an official statement.

But Mr X had always told Ivor that he'd been too scared to put himself on record, to sign an official statement. He had a family he was trying to protect. He knew these people's reputations and he didn't want to get on the wrong side of the ones who were left. But he wanted to help us.

With all these memories coming back so many years after the fact, it was a pity he refused to put it all in a statement to the police. It was a shame he didn't stand behind his assumptions and recollections. It felt like we had once again been led a merry dance. We could not and did not ignore these accounts. But unless police were given sworn statements, we knew it would remain gossip, at best.

We also received information from a lad that Kaley knew. He confided in her about a potential sighting of Nicky McNamara holding a youth up against a wall on Bars Hill. However, he too refused to give a statement to the police. The boy's name was Ed Weaver and he admitted he'd dealt drugs for Nicky back in the day. He said that Nicky was in the flat above the butcher's that night. He knew because he claimed he was there.

'He said that Damien had shouted up, "Have you got any pills?" and Nicky McNamara was fuming about it,' Kaley said. 'He went to another party later on and another lad came in and said he'd just seen Nicky beating the crap out of some kid.'

My heart began to race anxiously. Had Damien really been beaten up like that? Ed told Kaley that the lad who'd said it didn't know who the kid being battered was. But he knew Nicky, I thought.

'It was only over the next few days, when it came out that Damien was missing, that Ed and others at the party thought it might have been Damien,' Kaley explained. 'They told the bloke that claimed to witness it, and urged him to go to the police, but as far as Ed knows, he never did.'

All he knew now was that the guy was a window cleaner, living on the island. From our own investigations, we knew exactly who this guy was. Paul Foster. Back in 2005, he'd reported seeing the altercation. At the time he didn't think it had been Damien, but as time moved on, and with rumours abounding, a friend of his had suggested that it could have been Damien he'd seen being held up against the wall. Over time, both men had gone to the police and made statements. But what of this chap, Ed?

I shared the information with Liz Williams and asked if Ed had ever given a statement to the police. After a couple of weeks of chasing, I had an answer. He hadn't. They'd just had an informal chat with him. But there was no way for Ed to know that Paul was now a window cleaner unless he knew him. His story checked out.

To me it felt substantial, but the police didn't seem too bothered. In fact, unlike some of my other SIOs, it felt like Liz Williams was there just to field my questions, rather than push an investigation forward. Always busy with other crimes, murders and suchlike. There was no time for my Damien.

CHAPTER TWENTY-THREE

I‍T HONESTLY FELT LIKE OUR HANDS WERE TIED. WE HAD SO MUCH information but so many loose ends dangling. Yet we were getting minimal support from the police. In most cases, they'd simply look in Damien's files, tell us they had already spoken to the witness in question, and that was that. Even when the information deviated from what was previously heard, they refused to revisit the information. Or they would dismiss the source as not credible. Our efforts were becoming futile.

Then, just when I thought we had nowhere left to go, in August 2015 an email from a BBC reporter appeared in my inbox. Her name was Bronagh Munro, and she worked for the BBC's current affairs investigation team. At first I'd assumed it was just a simple request for an interview, until I read the email in full. It was actually much more than that.

'We would like to work with you and your family to discover if we could find further information that may help your family uncover where Damien is, and who is responsible for his disappearance,' she wrote.

I contacted her to find out more. She explained that the programme would be in the style of a Netflix documentary called *Making a Murderer*, just a more condensed version.

I'd never seen it, but had heard it was highly acclaimed. It was apparently about an unsolved case, much like Damien's in terms of the gossip and hearsay that surrounded it. I was intrigued. Once again I felt hope bubbling inside me.

Could this be it?

I knew that creating a piece of investigative journalism would be a lengthy and potentially intrusive process. Everything would be brought under scrutiny. But what did we have to lose? My thoughts on the matter were clear, but I couldn't make the decision alone. The family needed to agree too.

'What do you think?' I asked Ed and James at home.

'It sounds fantastic,' said Ed. 'It would be great to have fresh eyes looking at everything.'

James agreed. 'I'm up for it. What have we got to lose?' he said.

'They'll have an impartial view as well,' I enthused. I relished the idea of an investigation taking place that was outside the hands of Hampshire Police. It was all I had ever wanted – an independent review of the barrage of information we had gathered.

I spoke to Sarah and Melissa and they felt exactly the same. Even Ivor was on the same page as us. The only caveat laid down was that I speak on behalf of the family. The kids all had work commitments and families to support and Ed didn't feel comfortable getting in front of the cameras or being in the glare of the spotlight. Neither did I, but I'd been there for years. It was necessary to keep Damien's name out there.

After we agreed to participate, things moved quickly. The BBC team was keen for the documentary – which would be shown on its new online channel, BBC3 – to be broadcast ahead of Damien's nineteenth anniversary the following year.

We also had some more good news. After a difficult couple of years, Ivor was on the road to recovery and back on top form. He'd agreed to help us all he could with the investigation.

We handed over everything we could to Bronagh and her colleagues Alys Harte and Richard Parry. All the snippets of information, all of Ivor's statements and tapes from over the years, along with news cuttings and correspondence with police. Everything that I felt might help them understand how we'd got here and where we stood, almost nineteen years on from Damien's disappearance. Truth be told, I was worried the sheer volume would overwhelm them, but they took it in their stride. They were determined and relentless.

Two months after that first email, in October 2015, Bronagh, Alys and their crew moved over to live on the island to start their investigation. Once they'd settled in we chatted on the phone. Bronagh made sure to manage my expectations from day one.

'We don't know if we can solve this case, Val,' she said. 'But we'll look at everything and see what else we can find out.'

'Anything you can find will help us,' I said. I was so grateful for the opportunity. I tried to temper my excitement, but it was hard not to get my hopes up. The team had access to all kinds of resources we'd never had before – fully trained journalists with a police background and even cadaver dogs. As a BBC operation, everything had to be professionally executed. The team even offered to work alongside the ongoing police investigation and asked to film me at my next update meeting, which was due in January 2016. But the police refused any participation.

Surprise, surprise.

Quite frankly it was embarrassing that the force working with us wanted no part in the programme. I guess, in their eyes, the case was wound down and they didn't want anything to reinvigorate it. I truly believed they thought they'd finally rid themselves of Damien – the thorn in their side. Instead, they had to deal with a crack investigation team, a camera crew and an army of Damien's supporters.

The process was physically, mentally and emotionally draining. It felt like I gave every waking minute on the phone or email to Bronagh or Alys, recounting and rehashing all the information. Finding and sending emails and statements I'd collected over the years. I'd honestly believed I had all the details stored in my mind. But as they forced me to dig deep into my memory, I realised that wasn't the case any more. Each time they pulled at one thread, something long forgotten in the murky mist of memory would resurface, connected to another story or theory.

The questioning was relentless, to the point where the 'ping' of an email notification would cause a knot to form in my stomach. They were tough at every turn, but always genuine, tenacious and conscious of what a huge thing they were asking of my family and me.

They even took the time to film a candlelight vigil held by Lynn to mark the nineteenth anniversary of Damien's disappearance. At the heart of everything they did there was concern for us. For Damien.

And a relentless desire to get answers.

After they'd spent two months on the island, James flew back to the Isle of Wight from the USA to meet with them. The BBC team had asked to film him speaking with Chris Boon. It was a difficult and emotional decision, but James agreed to get involved. I couldn't have been more proud of him.

I'd heard that quite a few of Damien's friends had agreed to take part. The ones who had declined, I understood fully. They had never wanted to speak publicly. As well as being grateful to those who'd agreed to get involved, I was worried for them too. Would they be exposing themselves too much? They were all adults now, but I couldn't help but feel concern.

I travelled to Gloucester to spend Christmas with Nigel and the family but I wasn't due on the Isle of Wight for filming until January. While James was back on the island, I was at home, hard at work answering as many of Bronagh and Alys's questions as I could. The names of the people they were really probing into didn't surprise me at all: Mr X. Bunny Iles. Danny Spencer. Shirley Barrett. Nicky McNamara.

They were the same old pieces of the puzzle that we'd never managed to put together. Would Bronagh and Alys be able to crack it? Before I travelled, they prepared me for what to expect when I arrived.

'We're going to need you to be on call for us the whole time,' Alys said. 'We'll film some pieces with you directly, but we might need you to meet some people with us too.'

It turned out they'd also spoken to Mr X. They'd called him 'The Weatherman' due to the particularly dreadful weather one day when he agreed to meet Ivor and Lynn on a deserted beach on the island. It had been freezing and blowing a gale.

Apparently, he wanted to meet me and share his recollections face-to-face for the first time ever. It was something I was strangely looking forward to. This man had existed to me only in emails and through the accounts of people in my circle who had spoken to him. We'd never met in person. I wondered how I'd feel when we did. *Would I believe his account?*

'He might be a bit loud and erratic,' said Bronagh. 'He's very nervy. Are you sure you want to do this?'

'Yes, I do,' I said. I'd walk over hot coals if it would bring me closer to the truth.

When the time came, I sat with him in the BBC crew's car, the two of us alone but for the camera fixed firmly on my face. As he always had, he wanted to remain anonymous. He was so nervous and cautious that I couldn't help but ask, as the camera started rolling, 'Are you okay?'

'Yeah, fine,' he said. His expression said otherwise. I watched him as he regaled the tale of bumping into Nicky McNamara the day after Damien disappeared.

'He looked like a man fucked,' he said. 'Really fucked up in the head.' As he spoke about when he saw Nicky later that day, burning bits of wood in an old oil drum, his demeanour changed.

'There was enough time for me to see him come out with this fuckin' long black stringy thing that looked like it could have possibly been a sleeve,' he said, his voice cracking.

After circumnavigating the point for a few seconds, he continued. 'He simply looked like he had hold of an arm and he was about to go and drop it into the oil drum.'

It sickened me to think this might be what they had done to my lovely son, but I did my best to retain my composure.

'Mmm,' I said, squeezing my eyes shut for a moment. I had braced myself for hearing the worst and here it was. But I would not allow myself more than a momentary flinch. I needed to allow myself time to consider if what he said made sense. To see if I had doubts. I had learned over the years to hold fast and remain strong. I'd save the emotional unwind for when I'd had time to consider all the possibilities.

'I wanted you to tell me this face-to-face,' I said. 'It means a lot more to me than hearing it second and third hand.'

'I've waited a long time to meet you,' he said. I could tell the emotion in his voice was genuine.

'I appreciate you doing this,' I continued. 'I can see it weighs heavily on you.'

'The only way I can describe it is that it eats at your soul,' he said, before he crumbled, tears falling down his cheeks. He told me it had taken him so long to come forward in the first place because the 2011 searches had jogged his memory. 'I spent years not joining the dots,' he said.

It was so disturbing to hear that Damien might have been dismembered and burned. No matter how many times I heard these stories, I never became immune to the pain.

It was like someone tearing at my soul. After meeting Mr X in person, I thought that he was convinced he was telling the truth. I didn't think he was lying. Not for one second. He was telling us what he believed he had seen. But had his mind played tricks on him? He had no solid proof. What's more, he still refused to give this statement of accounts to police. So once again we were hearing unsubstantiated information and someone's opinion, not fact.

As I mulled over the other elements of his story that we'd

heard over the years, my thoughts focused once again on the CCTV footage. All this could have been so easily confirmed or denied by its existence. Instead it remained a question mark looming large over so many people. It had not only turned my life upside down, but also this man. A man with a family of his own. And God knows how many others.

* * *

I was well prepared for my meeting with Liz Williams. As well as my own long list of unanswered questions, which I always seemed to have on these occasions, Bronagh had added a few that had arisen from the BBC investigation. Despite myself and the BBC making the request, the camera crew was refused access to film the meeting. They wouldn't even allow a mocked-up version to be filmed, as they had in the past. They locked the BBC right out.

Me and my siblings, Nigel and Sally, went in for the meeting alone. Just being on those steps – the same ones I'd climbed that first night Damien had gone missing – brought terrible memories flooding back. The anxiety, the fear, the helplessness. Not to mention how heartlessly I'd been dismissed by the officers inside. My face must have said it all.

'Must bring back some bad memories,' Bronagh said.

'It really does,' I replied. It was right here on these steps that this horrendous journey had started. Almost twenty years ago I had knocked on this door feeling like I was reaching for a lifeline. I never could have imagined the shambolic roller coaster ride I was going to be taken on.

Bronagh stayed outside with the crew, but they didn't have to wait long at all. The meeting consisted mainly of me asking my questions and Williams telling me she'd get back to me on the majority of them. She was full of a cold, but had dragged herself in for the meeting. I was grateful for that. In all honesty, I felt sorry for her. She'd inherited this mess of a case like the officers before her.

From the family's point of view, I wanted to understand what her role was, as it had never been fully explained. And she didn't act like an SIO. She'd told me that she was our custodian and the person who would update us on annual DNA checks – the big batch report of remains matched against the DNA of missing people every year. This hardly seemed like the most dynamic role, even by her own description. That said, I was sure she'd be promoted or retired, like every other SIO that had ever been handed the case. Truth told, it was deeply disheartening, but all I could do was accept it. I brought up other, more pressing questions.

Bronagh and Alys were also hot on the heels of Shirley Barrett and were keen to learn more about an alleged 'deathbed confession' from Nicky McNamara. They'd wanted to know more about who had reported this.

'There are limitations around this,' Williams had said. Meaning she didn't want to comment on it, I guessed. Not wishing to flog a dead horse, I moved on to some questions about her current and former colleagues. We'd received numerous reports, including from Mr X, that some police officers had been in Damien's vicinity that night: one on the High Street near Yorkies; another who had spoken to the social worker waiting at the bus stop for his kids, just after he'd seen a youth he believed to be Damien. All we wanted was to make sure we had every shred of information and ensure that nothing had been missed.

'They should have police notebooks and rosters they can refer to,' Bronagh had said before I went in.

'I'll find out,' I promised. When I asked Williams, I was shocked by the response.

'All old police notebooks were destroyed,' she said. 'We maintain records digitally now.'

'So you don't have them?' I asked, for clarification.

'No,' she said.

Maybe I had watched too many police shows over the years, where they suddenly put two and two together using old information to solve a case. But if old information wasn't kept, how could that work? I tried another item from my list – the CCTV footage from Yorkies that had been spliced to edit out the police car. After being provided with another copy of the spliced version, I'd asked for a copy of the unedited video version.

'What about the footage from Yorkies?' I asked. 'I assume there *is* still a full unedited version?' On top of everything else, I wanted to make sure I still had a copy of every last snippet of my son. The footage was precious for so many reasons.

'I'll look into that for you,' she said. Fobbed off again, I thought.

As I went down my list, I felt we were going nowhere. She didn't seem to have a good handle on the case at all, and constantly needed to refer back to other officers who had worked on Operation Ridgewood. But the real kicker came when I asked about the status of the case.

'Is the case still being considered a suspected murder?' I asked.

'Oh no,' said Williams. 'The status of the case is the same as it's always been. A missing person case.'

'We were told by Heelan ahead of the arrests that it had been escalated,' I said. As the information slowly sank in, I felt deflated.

'It's always been a missing person case,' she continued, matter-of-factly.

I was past the point of wasting my breath to contest it. Once again I left with half a story and little faith. Bronagh was waiting by the door as we emerged.

'How did it go?' she asked. The cameras were rolling and all I could bring myself to do was shrug. What was there to say?

In the car we chatted some more, going over the basics of the meeting for the film. I was trying to remain calm, but as I spoke I could feel anger brewing inside me as I processed the meeting. So many questions unanswered. So many things referred back to previous investigating officers. I knew I'd hit the big blue brick wall yet again. How long would it take to get answers this time?

'If they'd done it right in the first place, I wouldn't be here now,' I said. 'My whole life's been turned upside down because of stupid people who couldn't do this right in the first place.'

I was still feeling totally frustrated and let down when I got back to The Fountain hotel, where we'd made our base, but I allowed the emotions to dissipate. Lots of people – my friends, Damien's pals and members of 'Team Damien' – had heard I was over and dropped by to say hello. While I was here I was going to make the most of seeing loved ones, having a catch-up with endless cups of coffee.

And feeling closer to Damien. I always did when I was on the island. It was like it connected him to me. I was in a place where he'd lived and laughed, a place where I could still feel him. The support and care from our friends and supporters there bolstered me too, for which I was eternally grateful. But I still didn't know what had happened to my son. I couldn't grieve like others did when a loved one had passed. There was no marker. Just a place where he'd been.

As the days passed, Bronagh asked me to retrace Damien's last-known footsteps with her, looking at where the CCTV cameras would have been and the things that had been happening nearby. Until that last shot of him, there had been practically minute-by-minute sightings of him for almost an hour as he'd moved around town. Then the sightings ceased, in the middle of a deserted high street.

He suddenly disappeared, never to be seen again, if you discounted the unconfirmed sighting on Baring Road, as the police had. Poor uptake on the lead had always left us wondering. It was like he had vanished off the face of the earth.

As we reached the bracket where the camera that captured the last glimpse of him used to be, we stopped. The town council had long since removed that camera. Some suggested it might have been removed because of the connection with Damien. It had negative connotations. *Bad for tourism . . .*

But I didn't care about all that. Standing on that very spot all I could remember was that grainy glimpse of his sweet face – happily eating his chips. I closed my eyes and grasped on to that memory. Remembered the feeling I'd had the night I'd seen the footage at the Marina. What I wouldn't give to have that footage now! Not for the investigation. Not for this film. For me. To treasure that last image of my son, my baby.

Everything about the trip was emotional and draining. James had mentioned that the filming with him and Chris Boon had been tough too, a little awkward with people watching and waiting for you to talk. Chris was fresh off a business trip and hadn't even been home to see his family. He'd been exhausted.

Waiting in The Fountain, I was wondering what I'd be asked to do next. I'd heard Bronagh and Alys had spoken to Shirley Barrett. She'd insisted she couldn't remember what she'd told police about Damien being picked up on Baring Road, and she'd refused to talk about Nicky McNamara's death. When the cameras were off she'd apparently admitted to both of them that she'd lied to police and been paid for it.

Said a lot about her character.

They'd also tracked Danny Spencer down to London. He'd been arrested in connection with Damien's disappearance in 2011 and his file had been referred to the CPS, but he'd been released without charge. Bronagh and Alys also discovered that he had allegedly seen copies of witness statements.

I was deeply shocked. No wonder people were reluctant to tell the police what they knew. Where were the rights for the victim in all this? It beggared belief. Bronagh confronted Danny about Damien and the fact he'd been found with police witness statements. He'd apparently denied it all, then shouted and screamed about how the 'Damien Nettles thing' had ruined his life.

How ironic! A man who I'd been told had openly and drunkenly bragged that he knew what happened to Damien and chanted, 'No body, no crime.' He had the gall to blame MY son for HIS misfortune? *My heart bleeds for you,* I thought, sarcastically.

The BBC team had blown me away with what they had achieved so far. But when they turned up back at 'base', I could never have guessed whom they'd be speaking to next. Or what they were about to ask me to do. I could tell from Bronagh's face, it was big.

'Val,' she said. 'We need you to come with us now.'

'Where to?' I asked.

'To Bunny Iles's flat,' she said. 'He's said that he'd like to speak with you. In person.'

CHAPTER TWENTY-FOUR

M Y HEART WAS POUNDING AS WE PILED INTO THE CAR AND RACED across town. I guess Bronagh and Alys didn't want to give him – or me – time to overthink the decision and potentially back out. To be honest, I was stunned and a little wary that he'd even agreed. He and Nicky McNamara were as thick as thieves. Like brothers, we'd heard. We'd learned they were at the heart of drugs trade in Cowes and Newport in the 1990s. They roamed the streets like they owned them – high on all kinds and wreaking havoc.

Just like Nicky, Bunny's name had been connected to Damien's disappearance for years. I knew the police had spoken to him on more than one occasion. There was no evidence that he had killed Damien, but did he know what had happened to him? I couldn't figure out what he had to gain by putting himself in front of a national TV crew and me. He'd remained silent on the matter for years. The BBC was getting quite the exclusive.

All manner of scenarios flashed through my mind during

that the two-minute drive. What could he possibly want to say to me? Did he have some information? Or did he just want to put distance between himself and Damien's story? Whatever it was, I was about to find out.

We pulled up outside an ordinary-looking house that had been converted into flats. Situated in an ordinary neighbourhood in Cowes, from the outside it looked like it could be the home of an ordinary person. But even based on second- and third-hand information, he was no ordinary man. He was the bogeyman in the background of so many stories we'd heard over the years. He had a nasty reputation for dealing drugs and threatening people. He commanded fear.

As we climbed the stairs, I felt myself tense up. I was nervous and worried about the precarious situation I was putting myself in. But it could be my last hope in making sense out of the rumour and speculation. Never in my life did I believe I would be coming face-to-face with a man like Bunny Iles. He'd been a renowned criminal, a drug dealer and a drug addict. It defied belief, really. How the heck did I get here? If I'd had longer to think about it, fear may have got the better of me. But the adrenaline had kicked in. Now here I was. Standing at Bunny Iles's front door.

Bronagh knocked and the door opened. There he was, bulky and tattooed, wearing a heavy silver chain. He still looked every inch the gangster. He towered over us at more than six foot tall. My palms became clammy and I felt myself start to shake. He'd aged from pictures I had seen in the past, but he was still intimidating. Not the kind of man you'd want to meet down a dark alley, that was for sure.

'Hello, Valerie,' he said with a nod, his gruff voice slow and purposeful. I was glad that he instinctively seemed to know to leave a respectful gap between us. Conflicting emotions simmered beneath my calm exterior. I wondered if he thought I would come in screaming and shouting at him. Or did he think I would berate him and his associates?

That wasn't my style. I would remain affable and dignified. I would hear him out. I wouldn't sink to that level. I simply nodded back in greeting.

As the team fitted me with my mic and set up the shot, Bunny made us all a cup of tea. I almost laughed out loud at the absurdity of it all. The man who'd spent years as a wicked and dangerous spectre in my mind was asking me if I took sugar.

'Okay, Val,' Bronagh said. 'We're almost ready. Take a seat here and we'll get started.'

'No problem,' I said, as I positioned myself on the sofa opposite where Bunny was sitting. Looking around the room, it was hardly the den of iniquity I'd expected. I absorbed the normality of it all: a well-worn green armchair that was clearly 'his' chair; silly little statues and knick-knacks, probably from holidays he'd been on; photos of his kids and family. It was a stark reminder of why I was here. For my Damien. My baby. I wanted to know what Bunny knew. I wanted to know if he thought his friends were capable of killing a young boy.

'I only heard the name Nicholas McNamara from the police after he died. Obviously you're friends with him, so your name got in the frame,' I began, firmly. But before I could even get my question out, Bunny started speaking.

'Look,' he said, his eyes locking with mine. 'I can one hundred and one per cent tell you that I know nothing about it, knew nothing about it, had nothing to do with it. I am ninety-nine point nine nine per cent sure that my best friends at that time, I do not think, had anything to do with it.'

I nodded and listened as he carried on in defence of his friends, saying that if they *had* done anything, then they had hidden it well from him.

'I defy anyone to do something like that and not change,' he said. 'It's impossible, Valerie, surely?'

Well, I was hardly going to agree with that, was I? He was better placed than I to know how people who did bad things justified it to themselves or others. He'd probably been doing it for years. From the stories I'd heard, it seemed they were capable of hiding all manner of despicable acts. Even to those closest to them. They were survivors. At anyone else's expense but their own.

The conversation continued. Bunny openly admitted that police had spoken to him four times about Damien, the last three properties he'd lived in had been searched, and he'd even been accused of turning up at the flat to dispose of Damien's body. Moira House, perhaps? Ivor had found further evidence that people had been living there from a man who had visited the address around the time of Damien's disappearance.

Or what about the flat over the butcher's? As Bronagh pushed the interview forward, Bunny told us how he'd operated his trade out of Fellows Road. He said that he and Nicky, along with the rest of their gang, had most of the clubs and pubs in Cowes and Newport 'sewn up' back in the day. Was that why we'd been met with so much reluctance and fear of speaking up when Damien first went missing? Did people know Nicky and his crew were involved and so kept their mouths shut? Bunny wasn't shy about his past, but when Bronagh hinted at the suggestion they'd sold drugs to kids of Damien's age, he point blank denied it. Said his gang didn't come into contact with many youngsters. He seemed to think his crew was too intimidating.

'Damien Nettles's name didn't come into our lives until the day we started getting arrested,' he said.

I felt confused and conflicted as I listened. He was affable, polite and had been respectful towards me. But over the years I had met and heard about so many people who lived in fear of Bunny, Nicky and their cronies. Learned of lives destroyed by the drugs they peddled. When Bunny talked about their posse running round off their faces doing 'crazy' things, I wondered if he cared at all about the trail of pain and destruction they had left in their wake. As our time drew to a close, Bunny made what felt like his final pitch to me.

'We never committed any murders or got rid of any bodies,' he said. 'That's all I can say, Valerie. Hope you believe me and I hope this does get solved.'

I didn't say whether I believed him or not, I just thanked him for his time.

'I really do appreciate you speaking to me,' I said, maintaining my distance from him. Being in such a small space with this notorious man who had occupied so much of my mind for many years was intense. The interview seemed to last a lifetime, but we were in there for less than an hour. As we emerged from the house and drove to the seafront, I'd barely had time to catch my breath before the camera was back on me, capturing my immediate reaction.

'Was that what you expected, Val?' Alys asked.

'It was what I hoped for,' I said calmly. 'He was amenable and very, very honest about his past.' What more could I say? I could barely believe what had just happened. I needed time to process it, to decide if I believed him or not.

* * *

From moving to the island to getting everything ready for the BBC Three broadcast took about eight months. Even after I returned home, I was responding to queries from Bronagh and Alys and making clarifications to their legal team. I was astounded by what they had managed to gather in a relatively short space of time.

They spoke to another PI, who had also heard stories about Danny Spencer swanning around town saying, 'No body, no crime,' and using vulgar language to describe my sweet boy. They spoke to an anonymous witness who claimed Nicky McNamara had been acting paranoid and shifty after Damien had disappeared. They also spoke to countless people about incidents that couldn't be broadcast for legal reasons. Every shred of what they found was handed to the police. I knew they were all a little disappointed not to have solved the case, or at least found something that moved it on further from where we were. I wanted them to know that the film had value even without that kind of conclusion.

'I'm amazed at how much you have done, whatever the conclusion is going to be,' I said in an email to Bronagh. 'It's going to be interesting to see how it's received.'

'I think the biggest impact will be shining a light on this case,' she replied. 'Highlighting what happened and perhaps what hasn't been done.'

I couldn't have agreed more. Finally, in July 2016, ahead of its launch, the BBC sent me the full series. I shared the file with the rest of the family, and then settled down to watch it at my computer, alone. I wanted to be able to absorb every single second of it. My body tingled with nerves and excitement as I hit 'play'. I knew from the buzz created by pre-publicity that the show had the potential to make a big impact.

Did I expect it to solve the mystery? Of course not. But I was sure as heck it would bring certain characters out of the woodwork. Put Damien back in people's minds. Up to this point I knew only whom the team had spoken to, and what had happened in the segments I had been filmed for. I was looking forward to seeing the finished article given how much time and effort our friends, family and supporters had put in to get it done.

I sat and watched all eight episodes back to back – two hours, like a feature-length film. Afterwards I was emotionally drained. From the actors filmed retracing Chris and Damien's footsteps on the night he disappeared, to Bronagh challenging Danny Spencer outside his London home, it was filled with highs and lows. I'd cried as Damien's friends had shared their memories of him; looking at old pictures and openly letting tears fall for their friend who never came home.

'He was exciting to be around, things would happen when he was there.'

'He was a gentle, beautiful person who wouldn't hurt a fly.'

That was the boy I remembered.

I'd shuddered as Lynn took Alys and Bronagh to the house where Damien had allegedly been killed. I felt physically sick as she recounted just one of the many theories we'd heard over the years – that Damien had angered the island's drug fraternity and been brought there to be taught a lesson. *Beaten and left to choke to death on his own vomit before being wrapped in a carpet and disposed of.*

I was disgusted by Danny Spencer's pitiful comments about a life ruined. But nothing hit me harder than the stories from Damien's friends. Stories about how this seedy, druggy world danced at the edges of their existence. How the island's poisonous side had somehow seeped into our world without us really knowing. It seemed that no matter who you were or what you did, you couldn't avoid these despicable people. You'd always rub up against people who knew people. The island – Cowes, in particular – was just too small.

Damien's younger brother James, ex-girlfriend Abbie, best friend Vicky and Chris Boon, who were nice kids from good families, had all come into contact with this underbelly. It saddened me that people like Bunny Iles and Nicky McNamara had preyed on the vulnerability of our youngsters. I was also a little shocked to be hearing some of their information for the very first time. Why hadn't they told me earlier? Told the police or mentioned it in statements? I knew teenagers had their secrets, but why didn't they feel they could tell me the things they had heard?

I don't think we, as the parents of four children, were ignorant of what teens were exposed to, but in 1996 we did not have any concept of the *extent* of the drug scene in Cowes and the Isle of Wight. The police knew. In hindsight, after hearing from several people in an age group that would have been at school around the same time as my kids, there was a prolific drug culture in Cowes at that time, and it beggars belief that this was not stopped by the authorities and, most specifically, by the police.

Back then, we were not aware that Damien had done anything other than smoke some pot and drink cider, and we still have no valid proof that he did so.

In reference to Damien's appearance in the Yorkies CCTV footage, I realise numerous people have said it looks like he was on drugs, but that still strikes me as off base. I was not personally aware of what effect any drug in particular would look like. I did recognise that he had been drinking because we know that for a fact, but I don't have the professional skills to eyeball a human being in a short piece of film footage and inflict an opinion about them publically. None of his friends gave a statement to police that he took drugs or had any connections to that circle. This is why some of the comments in episodes of *Unsolved* struck me as odd. Had the police been involved with the production, I would have expected them to re-interview those people thoroughly and ask why they saved those comments for the camera, and if they would be prepared to provide updated statements. However, the police stayed well away.

Part of me did wonder if Chris, in particular, was sure about some of the things he said in the show. James had said Chris had been exhausted the night they filmed their chat. Had the sleep deprivation made him confused? Was he recalling things accurately? But with the show finished and ready to go out, it didn't really make much difference. With all the information she had, Bronagh concluded that Damien *could* have come into contact with Bunny Iles at some point. Even fleetingly.

Despite my eyes having been opened to the scale of the drug problem for young people on the island, I wasn't so sure. I honestly believed that if he was going to smoke a little pot, there were much easier ways for him to come across it. Ways that didn't involve tangling with a man like Bunny Iles. What I *was* sure of was that Bunny Iles had been economical with the truth when he faced me in the interview.

Following the show I received message after message from people who had been around Damien's age when he and his cronies had been at the height of their criminal careers. They'd been in that house on Fellows Road – and others like it – and been provided with whatever drugs they asked for. One message came from a girl that Sarah had known at school.

'I'm ashamed to admit it now,' she said, 'but around that time I had made friends with the couple who lived in the chalet that was searched. Damien would have been aware of this and, if he wanted anything, he could have come to me. He didn't need to go to Bunny Iles or Nicky McNamara.'

I balled my hands into fists as the realisation sunk in. The local dealers were all interconnected. Bunny Iles had lived a long life of surviving. Spinning a story to stay out of trouble. And now I suspected that was exactly what he'd done at our meeting.

CHAPTER TWENTY-FIVE

IN THE DAYS THAT PASSED I LET THE FULL FORCE OF THE SERIES WASH over me. It took so many pieces of Damien's case and created a picture of the dangers that teens were being exposed to in 1996. But it was just one theory. The tip of a rotten iceberg.

I'd expected that the connection of the case with the island's drug fraternity would be the strand the BBC followed. My own conversations with the media had put that theory out there a long time ago – something I still cursed myself for. I couldn't blame them for picking up on it. It was possibly the most compelling theory we had, with the information that we possessed. But if Hampshire Police had done things the right way in the first place, acted faster or secured the High Street CCTV, maybe we'd have known more. That CCTV would have been a gift to any investigation, remember. They might have stopped us ever getting to this point.

I couldn't deny that some parts of the series made me uncomfortable. I wasn't sure if some of the drugs talk had been exaggerated for the cameras. If maybe people had said what they thought the BBC wanted to hear? I was also worried that Chris did not come over well. I wondered if it was fair to put him out there, to face any backlash, on the island or even online. Would he be able to cope? But after sharing my concerns with Bronagh, and watching it through again, I decided that if Chris was happy, then so was I. It was a *very* good piece of investigative journalism and it was going to put Damien back in the spotlight. That was all I ever asked for nowadays – for him to be remembered.

When *Unsolved: The Boy Who Disappeared* was finally broadcast online on BBC3, the response was phenomenal. It was clear that it left viewers with more questions than they started with, and reflected activities in 1996 that police would have been fully aware of. There was no neat ending. In fact there was no ending at all. There never would be, until we found Damien's body.

We understood that *Unsolved* might not bring us a conclusion. The clue was in the title, after all. But what the series did do was generate intrigue and give the case a real profile. As more and more people watched, the Damien Nettles Facebook group saw a huge jump in new members. Hundreds joined, most with good intentions, such as sharing new information, offering help and providing ideas about how we could move the case forward.

One woman, Caroline Lyons, who had tweeted and shared our posts for a long time, came forward with innovative ideas about using petitions to gain government support and even change policy. She was dedicated and warm and she was on our side. We quickly became firm friends. But others joined for different reasons: to keep an eye on us or to post nasty, offensive messages.

I'd always suspected that the programme would rattle some

cages, bring certain people out of the woodwork. I was right. In the days after the show aired, a threatening and abusive post in support of Nicky McNamara appeared on a public Facebook page. It was removed quickly, but not before Ivor found it and I took a screenshot.

> Who else wants to be buried never to be found again . . .
> You want to no [sic] what happened that night Come see me.
> I was with Nicky the night Damien died.
> R. I. P. TRUE LEGEND!!!!!!!

The post oozed bravado and pride at the poster's alleged knowledge of Damien's fate. It said little for his intelligence and mentality. Although this person hadn't been mentioned in the film he was quick to jump into some Facebook drama, squarely putting himself into the scene. When I read it I could feel my blood boiling. He was one of the lads who had been in the flat above the butcher's shop that night. One had to wonder how he knew Damien was dead. With that in mind, I passed the information to Liz Williams.

'He gave a statement years ago,' she said. 'This will not be revisited.'

It felt as though they could brazenly flaunt their knowledge with no fear of repercussions. They didn't care about what their words would do to us. In fact, they relished throwing salt in our open wounds. It wasn't an isolated case either. There were plenty just like him. Like the last two individuals arrested back in 2011. They'd too blasted the police and us on their Facebook pages.

Bottom feeders, that's all they were. The type of creatures that existed in the shadows, hidden under rocks, and only slithered out in the dark of night to distribute their poison and hawk their ill-gotten goods. Terrorising people and destroying lives. I know I was right because, after the show, people came right out and told me. Told me tales of addiction, violence and murder. It all came hand-in-hand with the island's bottom feeders.

My suspicions about Bunny Iles and his version of the truth were further confirmed too. More and more people, who had been children and teenagers when he, Nicky and their posse ruled the island's drug scene, came forward. They were adults now, with good professional jobs and families of their own. Many were ashamed of their past, but they wanted me to know that, back then, they'd taken drugs. And it was Bunny and his gang that had supplied them. They'd known how old they were and it hadn't stopped them. They didn't care.

As well as people reaching out to tell me their stories and share other information, the requests for media interviews flooded in too. For weeks I stayed up into the small hours of the morning to do breakfast news interviews in the UK. It was exhausting but worth it. For every uncomfortable question about Damien's possible relationship with drugs – which I believed had been blown out of proportion – there were ten about the police investigation.

Hampshire Constabulary had been conspicuous by its absence. The force hadn't even provided a statement to Bronagh and the team for the programme. It was only after the broadcast of *Unsolved* that the *Daily Mirror* managed to squeeze the most generic of responses from them. It read: 'Officers from Hampshire Constabulary's Major Crime team have watched the BBC3 online documentary about the case of missing Isle of Wight teenager Damien Nettles. Any information received following the programme will be assessed in due course in line with police procedures.'

Perhaps they thought it might all go away if they didn't engage. They should have known better by now. It made me even more determined to carry on and find answers, with or without them. To highlight just how poorly Damien's case had been handled.

Reviews of the series in national and even international publications were critical of Hampshire Police and its handling of the investigation. It finally felt like the injustice my family had suffered for nearly twenty years had found the platform it needed and deserved. It attracted the attention of just the kind of person we needed.

In October 2016 we learned that the story of our case had reached an esteemed London lawyer called Ian Brownhill. He was a human rights and public law specialist with a renowned firm and he wanted to help us. The team that supported Kerry Needham, the mother of missing toddler Ben Needham, had introduced us. He'd worked tirelessly on a pro bono basis for the Needhams alongside South Yorkshire Police, who had gone above and beyond to help her in her search.

A stark contrast to our experience.

He'd supported Kerry in her campaign to secure £700,000 from the then Home Secretary, Theresa May, to allow investigations to continue into Ben's disappearance. Now Ian wanted to help us. He wanted to make sure that Damien's case received the attention and investigative resource it deserved. That it wasn't forgotten. We were thrilled to have him on board as part of 'Team Damien'. His observations on the case and the outpouring of support following the broadcast of *Unsolved*, combined with the perturbing lack of communication from DI Williams, spurred me into action.

'It is with great sadness I feel compelled to submit another formal complaint with grievances in the way my son's case has been and continues to be handled twenty years on,' I typed. What followed was a comprehensive document succinctly outlining every single one of the force's failures. It challenged their failure to meet professional standards, take due care with vital evidence, keep accurate records and treat my family and my missing boy with the respect we deserved.

The twentieth anniversary of Damien's disappearance was marked with a reconstruction of his last-known movements by Lynn, her family and our supporters. We also launched another appeal, not just for new information but for funding too. We'd so often been told that a lack of resources and money prevented Damien's case from being elevated, that we decided to try and find a solution. We knew that to stand any chance of finding him, we would need the forensics and cold case murder teams.

Expertise like that cost money. Money that Hampshire Police said it didn't have. So, just as the McCanns and Needhams had done, we petitioned the government to provide funds for Hampshire Constabulary to continue Damien's investigation. The Madeleine McCann inquiry received an extra £12 million, while Ben Needham's case received an additional £1 million. Surely Damien's case deserved the same level of intervention?

'If the money is there, what excuse will Hampshire Police have?' I said to Ed.

'None at all,' he replied.

Or so you would think . . .

Bolstered by Ian's expert guidance and high media profile, and with the help of our loyal supporter, Caroline Lyons, we promoted the petition, generating plenty of media coverage. We needed 10,000 signatures to receive a government response and 100,000 for the petition to be considered for debate in Parliament.

In its first few weeks the petition rapidly gathered around 3,500 signatures. Our faithful local media threw their weight behind it too. But the voices of authority on the island stayed silent. Hampshire Constabulary offered no support despite the fact that the petition directly requested additional financial support for their own operation. I was once again disappointed and baffled by their attitude. When Kerry Needham had issued her petition, South Yorkshire Police had stood with her and supported her. It was a united front with one goal. They wanted to solve the case. I couldn't help but wonder how it must look for our petition not to have the backing of the investigating force. Was it them who looked bad? Or us?

'Why on earth would they not support this petition?' I said to Caroline, utterly frustrated for her as much as myself. She was the one who had worked tirelessly to compile and promote it.

'Maybe because they don't want it to succeed,' she replied. It certainly felt that way. All they ever seemed to do was work to shut us out. Even the clout of a heavyweight London lawyer didn't seem to budge them. Their communication with Ian had been minimal. At first, we thought delays in response might be down to the fact that DI Williams had been moved on from the case. But the silence continued even after our new SIO, DI John McGonigle, was appointed. He'd dictated that our only communication would be via the generic 'Operation Ridgewood' email, which he said he would review every two weeks. Often it was much longer.

Another wave of bad news landed too. I was informed that my second complaint had been handed back to Hampshire Police for a local investigation. Once again the force was tasked with scrutinising itself. I could already see the outcome. It would be in their favour, no doubt. As if that wasn't enough of a setback, despite all of our best efforts the parliamentary petition stalled at just short of 8,000 signatures and, in February 2017, it was closed. I was deflated. After all the attention that *Unsolved* had drawn, I was convinced we'd be able to make the 10,000 signatures mark at least.

'Where do we go from here?' I said to Caroline. 'What more can we do?'

'There must be something,' she said.

'We've tried everything,' I sighed.

Our despair and disappointment was only further compounded by the outcome of the local investigation. The force upheld a number of our complaints. They agreed that the missing person procedure had not been adequately followed early in the investigation, from the slow response and their dismissive attitude to me, to vital CCTV footage being lost or spliced without a copy of the original being saved. They also agreed that the force had failed in its duty by not identifying the other army men in Yorkies for fourteen years, despite it being a priority recommendation in DCI Kilbride's 2007 review. In fact it upheld a number of discrepancies between what he recommended and what actually happened.

They even upheld my complaint that Damien's case wasn't

entered into HOLMES database despite the system being available ten years before he went missing. It took until 2002 for Hampshire Police to make use of it. Even then they didn't record information for earlier in the investigation. Another opportunity missed. No one would be held accountable, though. The passage of time apparently meant that they couldn't identify who had made the decision to not use HOLMES from the start. We would never find out.

But I wasn't satisfied with the outcome. They didn't uphold our complaint about the fact that the police didn't check the council's perception that Moira House had been empty for refurbishment at the time Damien went missing, or consider our evidence to the contrary. Nor did they consider the destroyed police notebooks to be an issue.

'They have said that because Damien's case wasn't considered a criminal matter at the start, there was no obligation for police notebooks to be kept,' I told Caroline, completely exasperated.

'How can that be right?' she said.

'They said that the process wasn't as rigorous back then as it is now,' I sighed. That wasn't any good for Damien. Nor was the response to our complaints about potential suspects not being properly investigated and witnesses whose evidence we felt had not been duly considered – the ones that officers had deemed unreliable, mentally deficient or branded just plain liars. A long list of names and not one credible witness among them? That jaundiced and arrogant attitude towards island residents always dumbfounded me.

'You have to take this to the IPCC,' Caroline said to me. 'This has gone on for too long.'

'I don't know if I have the energy anymore,' I said.

'You do, Val,' Caroline insisted. 'Look how far you've come. Look at everything you've done to keep this case alive.'

'I don't know . . .' I said.

'Do it, Val,' she urged. 'Do it for Damien. Do it for other families of missing people. I'll be right with you.'

I sucked in a deep breath. She was right. Why should I back down to the island's big blue brick wall now? No family should ever have had to go through what we had. We'd turned to the police at a time of need and they had let us down. We couldn't change what had happened to us, to Damien's investigation. But we could try to make a stand and demand changes that would hopefully stop it happening again.

That could be Damien's legacy.

'Okay,' I said with a smile and steely determination. 'Let's do it.'

EPILOGUE: DAMIEN'S LAW

ALMOST TWENTY-THREE YEARS HAVE PASSED AND DAMIEN STILL hasn't come home for tea. We have lived twenty-three years without his beaming smile and silly jokes. Twenty-three years without his creative flair and loving personality. For twenty-three years this planet has been poorer without his presence. As a family we wonder who he might be now. What he would have achieved with his life.

As a mother, there is an unending ache in the space where he should be. It hurts deep in my soul. We miss him every single day, far more than any of us can put into words. Since the night I first climbed those steps at Cowes Police Station, sobbing as I reported my sixteen-year-old child missing, a total of 1,134 people have been involved in the investigation, according to Hampshire Police. That includes investigators, witnesses and people of interest.

In the years up to 2013, 357 witness statements had been taken, yet Hampshire Police had deemed few of those witnesses

273

credible. Eight people were arrested in connection with his disappearance and suspected murder. All were eventually released without charge. Those are the 'official' figures.

Yet I, my family, Ivor, members of 'Team Damien' and the team behind BBC3's *Unsolved* have been provided with hundreds upon hundreds of other accounts not included in these figures. Twenty-three years and all of this information, yet we still have no conclusion. That is what hurts the most. Without concrete evidence all we can do is speculate about everything that might have happened. Of course, we press on. Why? Because we know the answer is out there. We know Damien's remains are out there and we will not rest until we find them.

This book spans twenty-three years of my life. I know that by telling the story of this chapter of my life, a picture has emerged that points a finger at the Isle of Wight's drugs fraternity – that one per cent of bottom feeders who sully a place of beauty. Did the island's shady characters play a part in my boy's disappearance? Were they the only ones involved? We may never know. There are other compelling theories that could not be included in this book due to legal restrictions, many intricately intertwined into the island's interconnected bloodlines – families and friendships that straddle both sides of the law. One day, one of these stories may reveal itself to be the truth.

To those who know what happened to Damien and where he is now. To those of you who played a part. To those of you who will not implicate yourselves to give our family the peace of finding our son and laying him to rest, I have this to say:

I know you are watching. I've seen you, lurking in the comments on social media. I know you're looking to see how much we've learned. How close we are.

You're a parent now. You have a spouse and kids that trust you. Look at their faces, acknowledge the ferocity of the love you feel for them. I know the feeling. I have it for my own. *All of them.* Now imagine what *you* would do if what happened to Damien happened to them? Would you stop looking? Fighting?

I didn't think so.

Imagine now if your little brood found out about what you did back then. They don't know, do they? You've left that part of your life behind. What would they think if they knew? Would they still look at you in the same way? You've buried it all for so long, just like you did Damien's body.

Maybe you cleaned yourself up, got a decent job and a house. Moved on. Or at least tried to. But you can't run away from the things you saw, did or covered up, can you? They're etched in your mind. Like us, you can *never* escape what happened.

When the day comes that Damien is found – and that day *is* coming – it will be a bittersweet relief for my family. A chance to lay our sweet boy to rest, like he deserves. But your world will come crashing down. Just like ours did on that windy, rainy night in November 1996. Believe me, Damien's remains will talk.

I will go to the ends of the earth to find my sweet boy. To bring him home and have a marker. A place where I can go to him and be with him is all I want now. To find out who was responsible, but still have no body, would bring me no peace. I just want my Damien back. Like I have done since the night he disappeared, seemingly into thin air.

So much of the disappointment and anger I feel today is directed towards the failures of Hampshire Constabulary, which I consider to be unforgivable. From the very start their investigation was a shambles. Vital missing person procedures were not implemented and, as a result, critical evidence may have been lost. There was a lack of interest from local police about a missing teenage boy whom they dismissed as simply running away and having a 'funny five minutes'. They told me he'd be back by teatime, but I'm still waiting. They were so uninterested that they even got his age wrong, thinking he was nineteen – an adult – for the first week of the investigation. We'll never know what impact that could have had on the case.

Nor will we ever know what the lost CCTV footage of the High Street or the destroyed police notebooks might have told us. DCI Kilbride's words on this matter still stick with me today: 'That footage would have been a gift to any investigation.'

The litany of errors and miscommunications, lack of care and lack of interest over the past two decades beggars belief. It was more than *fourteen years* before any arrests were made – arrests prompted at least in part by information the force had been given in the days after Damien vanished. Potential witnesses not identified for more than *fourteen years*. CCTV footage was spliced and original versions lost. All of this has contributed to where we are now.

It could have been so different.

I realise now, after years of working alongside families of the missing, that not all cases are poorly investigated. However, many are and it is not good enough. Looking at other forces, providing caring and considerate FLOs to families, participating fully in TV documentaries like *Unsolved*, backing petitions and standing shoulder to shoulder with other families of the missing, I can do nothing but wonder what Hampshire Police has to hide.

Today, Damien's case is a cold case, sitting with Hampshire Constabulary's Missing, Exploited and Trafficked team. I have no real point of contact; even the generic 'Operation Ridgewood' email address is now defunct. I had my first annual cold case review in June 2019. We made an agreement to speak at six monthly intervals and that I would continue to receive annual updates on DNA – to identify if any remains with DNA matching Damien's have been found. The cold case team will also update me if there have been any new leads and they have assured me that they are open to communication should I have any information or questions. It's reassuring to have a point of contact. However, I still fear that one day, because of this cold case status, we will miss a vital witness. I feel that at every turn Hampshire Police have done their best to shut Damien's case down, silence it. Why? Is it trying to cover up its failings? Protect one, or more, of its own? One can only speculate.

Some of my complaints over the years have been upheld and the police have assured me they have learned some important lessons from Damien's case. When I am faced with such a statement, I cringe. What makes them think this offers any comfort? That Damien was some practice piece for them to learn from and improve their case management. What good do they think 'we'll do better next time' does for us? Or for Damien. For years the police have told us that they will only deal in facts. Well here are some facts to chew on:

Fact: on a cold, wet November Saturday in 1996, a nice ordinary boy went out to the small town of Cowes. He had a drink and was seen hanging out in an area less than fifty metres in either direction. Most accounts said he was in good spirits.

He bought some chips in a shop surrounded by army men and started making his way home. But he never made it. He disappeared from view at 12:02am.

Fact: in the days that followed, Hampshire Constabulary spectacularly dropped the ball, losing valuable time and opportunities to find Damien.

Fact: as a result our family has been torn asunder with grief and despair.

Fact: much of the information around what happened that night is gossip and speculation.

Fact: Damien is still missing and we will continue to fight to find him.

I am still angry, but I now channel my anger and frustration about this in a different way. As we compiled the IPCC appeal, Caroline and I also started work on something else. An idea that would take twenty-three years of pain and trauma and transform it into something positive and far-reaching. Something that would create a legacy from Damien's short sixteen-year life: *Damien's Law*.

It was an idea that sprung from the increasing realisation that we were not the only family suffering in this way, living a life of doubt and ambiguous loss as missing person cases go cold. There are thousands like us, struggling to cope with the aftermath of a person going missing alone. No body to bury. Unsure if they should mourn.

We have watched with concern over the years as the missing issue has grown, in particular the alarming amount of young men going missing on nights out. We have seen the imbalance in the attention that different cases get, with the lion's share of resources and media coverage going to missing girls and young children. Of course that level of attention is entirely warranted, but the same should be true for our teenage boys and young men.

Damien's Law seeks to challenge the perceptions of a lads' night out. To make sure that the risks of young men going missing after a night out with pals are acknowledged, especially if their families say the behaviour is out of character.

In 2017 Caroline and I created a petition, with guidance on the language we should use from the Missing People charity. It was the first iteration of Damien's Law. Our manifesto asked the following:

- All missing under-18s assessed for the Child Rescue Act.
- Risks associated with being missing on a night out acknowledged.
- Concerns of families to be taken more seriously.
- Specialist risk assessment training regarding missing person cases for police officers.
- Search teams deployed as soon as possible for medium- and high-risk cases.
- Greater transparency in how police allocate resources.

If these six simple points had been implemented in Damien's case, I am sure we wouldn't be here now. Our petition quickly gained support from notable figures including Ann Coffey MP and Charlie Hedges, a respected ex-police officer who is very active in his work around the missing issue.

We still require more signatures to get Damien's Law in front of Parliament, but already we are seeing changes. Charlie

Hedges has constructed learning modules in collaboration with Missing People to train police officers, first responders, the CPS, child services, foster carers, organisations dealing with mental health and other agencies involved in missing cases. It is this kind of education that will stop people like my Damien falling through the bureaucratic gaps.

While these are positive steps forward, there is much more to be done. Our petition remains open and we have a long-term vision to create a Centre of Expertise, where training around missing person cases and the care of their families could come together. For now we continue to push for support. We keep a spotlight on other missing person cases through our Missing Persons Support Facebook page and Twitter account by sharing information, in particular around older cases that no longer grab the media spotlight.

Nothing will ever, ever heal the pain of losing Damien. Ed, Sarah, James, Melissa and I will search for him as long as we have breath in our bodies – that is for certain. But we also want to ensure that no family ever has to endure the avoidable additional pain and trauma that we have suffered.

Finding our boy will be our resolution. The rest will be Damien's legacy. At times it is hard to maintain momentum. Sometimes it feels like we are getting nowhere and I want to stop and quit. I'm tired. But then, out of the corner of my eye, in the periphery of my vision, I see him – a tall, gangly lad with a sweet smile.

'Don't give up on me, Mum,' he says softly.

And I never, ever will.

ACKNOWLEDGEMENTS

Writing a book isn't something I ever thought would happen. I have always written things since I was young, putting pen to paper to express my thoughts, almost like a journal. Not every day, but when things were hard to fathom or deal with, I put it on paper. It was natural to do this again when Damien went missing. Trying to make some sense, as if writing it down I would suddenly see something I missed and it would all come together and be solved.

I have so many people to thank that I am sure I may forget someone – so to everyone who may have supported and helped us in any way – we are so grateful.

I thank my mother for passing on her love of writing and my Dad for his encouragement that me and my siblings could do more in life if we wanted it bad enough and put in the effort. He had a deformed left hand and became a design engineer. He beat that impediment, not always happily, but he showed us he overcame it and went on to work for NASA on the space

THE BOY WHO DISAPPEARED

shuttle design team. He did not happily see himself as a role model, but as kids and onlookers we saw how adversity could be overcome.

To my husband, Ed and my children Sarah, James, Melissa and their families. I have not always been fully focused on them since Damien vanished but they have always pitched in and helped and supported each other, while trying to make sense of their own loss. This kind of loss will devastate you or make you stronger. Our kids turned out to be strong people, survivors.

My siblings Nigel and Sally-Anne and their families. Thank you for all your support after Damien went missing and that you continue to provide. They have done fund raisers for Missing People Charity in Damien's name and attended events that I was unable to attend. Always and forever I am grateful for you all. Sophie, you have been a trooper from day one. It was actually on your birthday that Damien vanished, so every year it is a sad reminder for you on your special day. You have done so much to highlight the case over the years. Visiting the island to raise awareness or by fundraising, and supporting Missing People Charity with the amazing walk you did on the Isle of Wight. You are amazing.

Thanks to Ivor for stepping forward to offer help in the capacity of private investigator. A colourful character who I have thoroughly enjoyed knowing, with many a story to illustrate a point. Savvy, streetwise and a bulldog, his eye for the truth is sharp as a tack. You have encouraged me for many years to write a book and here it is. Thanks also to Caroline, without whom this book would not have been sewn together. Thanks for believing in me and pushing me to consider the possibility. Without both of you it may never have happened.

Carmelle, thanks for your faith, Damien was out there somewhere which was hope that we clung to for a long time. Corran, without your tenacity and your drive and your discovery of information, we may never have discovered the tape in the chip shop or found the impetus to push the powers to take notice of us.

Team Damien – Lynn, Kaley, Paula, Lyn, Andy, and the rest of the team who stoically and heroically continued to dig in all weathers. Their commitment to Damien was solid. I cannot begin to thank you all enough. They slipped and injured themselves and made themselves ill at times. They took time away from their own families and in all weathers continued to dig. Thank you to Mark and Vicky for allowing them onto your property to try and get some answers in our search for Damien and for joining in that search too. To all the friends and community on the Isle of Wight who rallied around our family in the early days and who continue to keep us in their hearts. Thank you. All the friends of Damien and their parents who scoured Cowes in that first search in November 1996. Thank you to all Damien's friends who have come forward with such touching memories of Damien. It is always good to hear those stories and to know he is still remembered fondly.

March for the Missing 2008, Nicki and Jill, we were amazing! Karen and Kathy thanks for the support of the former advocate group Forever Searching. You made a difference. Matt Searle MBE and Missing Abroad, thank you for stepping up and helping us get posters done for the march.

To some of the officers of Hampshire Constabulary who vainly attempted to rectify some major issues and who have over the years said they wished they could 'be the one' to crack this case. I believe you truly meant it. Thanks, Ian Brownhill, for your compassion and support and for trying to move a mountain. We appreciate your input and your help.

Thank you to Missing People Charity (formerly National Missing People Helpline) who I called the very next day after Damien vanished as I realised the police seemed unconcerned and we were up against something massive and devastating. They were a calm voice in a churning sea of despair and desolation. They provided us a platform for media and helped get the word out that our son was missing. They were and still are a huge support to families like mine who are experiencing this kind of ambiguous loss. Thank you for being there and for the amazing work and research that you carry out in the world of the missing.

BBC Three, Bronagh, Alys, Rich and Harry. Thanks for your valiant uptake on the information that we had at our disposal and which had left us weary and wondering what we were dealing with. You gave us the frank truth in the beginning with no promises, but a hope that something would come from all the leads. Taking the bull by the horns and delving into each and every aspect of the information we had and pursuing it hard to the end.

To old and new friends, thank you, we are in awe of the mark Damien left on the wider community.

Gone but never forgotten.

RESOURCES

UK Missing Persons Unit
Police resource linking to international missing persons organisations
https://www.missingpersons.police.uk/en-gb/international-organisations

Missing People (UK)
116 000 - free and confidential 24/7 helpline
https://www.missingpeople.org.uk/

National Missing Persons Helpline (Ireland)
Organisation supporting the families of missing people
http://www.missingpersons.ie/

Centre for the Study of Missing Persons (University of Portsmouth)
http://www2.port.ac.uk/centre-for-the-study-of-missing-persons/

The Samaritans
https://www.samaritans.org

Lucie Blackman Trust
Supporting British victims overseas
https://www.lbtrust.org

Charlie Hedges Advisory
Missing, Abducted, Trafficked Children and Adults
https://charliehedgesadvisory.com/

Crimestoppers
To report a crime anonymously, call: 0800 555 111
http://www.crimestoppers-uk.org/

ALSAR
List of search and rescue teams in the UK
https://www.alsar.org.uk/search-and-rescue-teams-in-uk/

UK Search and Rescue Framework
https://www.gov.uk/government/publications/search-and-rescue-framework-uksar

Children's Society
Information on 'county lines' and criminal exploitation
https://www.childrenssociety.org.uk/what-is-county-lines

Salvation Army
https://www.salvationarmy.org.uk/

The Big Issue
https://www.bigissue.com/about/

Centrepoint
Support for homeless young people
https://centrepoint.org.uk/

INTERNATIONAL

Missing Children Europe
http://missingchildreneurope.eu/

National Center for Missing & Exploited Children (US)
http://www.missingkids.org

Missing People Canada
http://missingpeople.ca/

International Centre for Missing & Exploited Children
https://www.icmec.org

FURTHER INFORMATION ON THE DAMIEN NETTLES CASE

Damien Nettles Website
Latest news, campaigns and links to relevant social media channels
Damiennettles.uk

Damien's Law
Petition created to get Damien's Law in front of Parliament
https://www.change.org/p/introduce-damien-s-law-with-improved-guidelines-to-ensure-more-missing-people-are-found

BBC 3: Unsolved: The Boy Who Disappeared
https://www.bbc.co.uk/iplayer/episodes/p060mvz3/unsolved